RETIRE YOUR WAY

DON'T JUST DREAM ABOUT RETIREMENT. PLAN FOR IT.

LOREN MERKLE
MERKLE RETIREMENT PLANNING

Loren Merkle/Merkle Retirement Planning
1860 SE Princeton Dr., Grimes, Iowa 50111
merkleretirementplanning.com

Book layout ©2023 Advisors Excel, LLC

Retire Your Way/Loren Merkle.

ISBN 9798393413040

"A goal without a plan is just a wish."

~ Antoine de Saint-Exupéry

Table of Contents

The Power of Planning

Fifteen dollars. Today, that's basically a ballpark beer, right? Maybe it's the lunch special at your favorite eatery. Perhaps a quarter tank of gas (okay, half a tank if you own a compact).

Let's face it, fifteen bucks just doesn't buy much these days. But forty years ago, fifteen dollars quite literally was everything to me—and it represented the price tag of one of the most influential lessons of my young life.

Before we get to that, let me start by noting that my childhood was pretty great. Growing up about five miles outside the nearest town of Central City, Iowa, life may not have been idyllic, but it provided a lifetime of incredible memories and shaped me into who I am today.

With our closest neighbor nearly a mile away, my three siblings and I basically had free run of the land that accompanied the farmhouse our parents rented. So long as we had successfully completed our daily chores, we'd play outside all day, checking in with our folks intermittently at best.

We'd build makeshift ramps for our bikes; strike up baseball, football, and basketball games, or play kick the can at night. During the winter, we even donned skates and tried to turn a ten-foot farm tractor puddle into our own personal ice skating rink. Basically, we'd do anything to stay outdoors and on the move.

But for all the fun I had at home with my older sister, older brother, and younger brother, some of my favorite memories came from our summer vacation trips to northern Michigan. We would tent camp about thirty miles north of Mackinaw City. For a kid who couldn't get enough time outdoors or with his family, those camping trips were formative enough that they still flood me with feelings of nostalgia.

Which brings me back to those fifteen dollars. To this day, I still remember the trip when I lost my wallet while playing on the trails. I searched for that missing treasure the entire rest of the week, then resumed my quest every time we returned to the campsite in subsequent years.

You see, when I lost that wallet, I didn't just lose the fifteen dollars it contained. I lost three months of hard work—ninety or so days of doing the family dishes, burning trash, vacuuming the house, cleaning my room, etc.—and the sense of accomplishment that accompanied my diligence. To a seven-year-old making five whole dollars a month for chores, that loss was devastating. Four decades later, I still occasionally find myself thinking about that darn wallet.

****

That's the thing about losses: They hurt, sometimes deeply. Whether you're a child who loses fifteen dollars, a promising young athlete who falls short in a key game, an accomplished business professional who is the unfortunate victim of staffing cuts, a son or daughter coping with the death of a parent, or a retiree who sees his life savings slashed by a market downturn, losses can be life changing.

Part of my "why" in becoming a retirement planner and founding Merkle Retirement Planning is to help people avoid the heart-wrenching types of financial losses I just mentioned. I want them to be as carefree and confident during retirement as I was as a kid playing in the Iowa sun. I want to help them retire their way by creating strategies that allow them to take ownership of the future and confidently pursue their dreams.

The other part of my "why" is that I understand what it means to work hard for what you've achieved and amassed. As you may have gleaned from the wallet story, my family wasn't wealthy. Raising a daughter and three sons who were separated by less than five years in age simply wasn't easy for my parents. My dad was a car dealership sales manager. My mom was a homemaker who later worked a variety of part-time jobs (school secretary, retail store employee, school bus driver), She eventually put herself through nursing school and realized her dream of becoming a registered nurse.

My parents inspired and motivated me—they still do—and I will always respect and appreciate the sacrifices they made to give their children the best chance to live full, fruitful lives. Still, I remember my friends spending a hundred dollars or more on a pair of Air Jordan basketball shoes. Luxuries like that weren't even a consideration in my house.

And that early 1900s farmhouse we rented? If it weren't for a few stubborn flakes that refused to relinquish their grip, the house would have appeared virtually paint-free. As I grew older and more conscious of the world and its wealth, my self-confidence sometimes resembled our house's weathered siding. It was fading at best. Each day as the school bus picked me up and dropped me off, I was attacked by feelings of insecurity, knowing that my peers had a front-row view of our haggard house.

Whether my feelings were justified or not, they fueled me. It was during my middle school years when I first vowed to figure out the world of money—how to make it, how to save it, and how to use it to enjoy a life of financial freedom and security. I didn't have the faintest idea how I would accomplish this; I just knew that would be my mantra moving forward.

****

As my fiftieth birthday creeps closer and closer, let me reiterate what I suggested at the outset: If I could redo my childhood, I wouldn't change much. With plenty of encouragement from my folks, my early years allowed me to immerse myself in numerous activities—I played football, baseball, and basketball, ran track, and played the drums in my school's marching, concert, and jazz bands. Those years also gave me skills I use today: The value of preparation, and how to be focused and present during a task at hand. This time in my life gave me the purpose that eventually became my life's mission to help others as a financial advisor.

Those years gave me power too, because in discovering the world of money, I developed muscles that turned weaknesses into strengths. For instance, I developed the muscles of:

- **Hard work** — To build wealth
- **Discipline** — To save what I work diligently to earn
- **Knowledge** — To grow money and use it to live well
- **Generosity** — To support the people and purposes I care about the most

This didn't happen overnight, of course. It was a long, arduous process, one that never will be completed. I'm still growing, still learning, and still striving. But what I have realized along the way is that this quest no longer is just about me. It's about others.

I want to help people travel, train, volunteer, golf, learn a new skill, pursue a new hobby, and chase their grandkids. I want to make sure they're overjoyed, not overwrought, every time the bus pulls up to their house. I want to help guard them against excess anxieties that make retiring stressful and much less enjoyable than it should be. And I want to guide them on their journey to a retirement filled with all of the confidence and excitement they have always dreamed of. The bottom line is this: Just as surely as I once so desperately wanted to find that wallet, I now want to help you find the financial confidence you may have lost. I want to empower you to retire your way!

****

The thing you may be saying to yourself is, "That's great, Loren, but how do you go about doing that?"

The answer, in a word, is planning. To achieve the retirement of your dreams, you don't need to find the perfect product or reach a certain financial threshold. You need to implement a prudent plan.

One of the most-asked questions my team and I get is, "How much do I need to retire?" Or, another version of this question is "How much do I need to ensure I won't outlive my money?" The problem with these questions is the answer can vary greatly depending on where you look. A while back, for instance, I read an article that said $3 million is the new $1 million when it comes to retirement funding. Another article indicated that $5 million could be a reasonable retirement price tag considering our nation's soaring inflation and national debt.

If those numbers scare you, I've got good news: The simple truth is that there isn't a magic, one-size-fits-all number for every person or family. Every year, our Merkle Retirement Planning team helps clients with $500,000 or less retire confidently and comfortably, fully ready to pursue their goals.

Unfortunately, we also have had to tell other families, who came to us with substantially more money, that it could one day run out because their strategies lacked reliable income streams and failed to account for lavish wish lists. The reality is that an individual or family could have a $5 million portfolio and still find their retirement in potential peril if they lead a lifestyle disproportionate to their means. .

Retirement, you see, isn't so much about the wealth you *attain* as the wealth you *retain*. It's about making sure you have a plan that includes strategies and products that provide reliable income after those steady paychecks—the ones that have been hitting your bank every week or two for the past thirty, forty, even fifty years—stop arriving. It's about protecting and possibly even growing your wealth without assuming unnecessary, uncomfortable, or unwise risk. It's about decreasing your retirement tax bill, optimizing your Social Security benefits, making prudent Medicare election choices, and ensuring all of this and more is working in tandem to provide you with your desired retirement lifestyle through building and implementing your custom retirement plan.

****

Sometimes, it's also about putting dreams on hold.

Not long ago, my team and I started working with a couple in their early sixties. Their previous advisor had told them that they could retire at the end of the year with a 99 percent probability of living the retirement they'd long envisioned. Good thing they sought a second opinion! When we put together our plan and performed our analysis, we found that they likely would have run out of money by the ages of seventy-five and eighty, respectively. Needless to say, they were shocked and visibly dismayed that their retirement dreams would have to wait a while longer.

But you know what? They also were relieved to discover the news then rather than five or ten years *after* they had retired, when their job prospects would have diminished significantly.

Yes, the news meant that they must continue working. Yes, their retirement journey would be a bit more winding than they initially thought. Yes, it was difficult and disappointing to hear. But they truly appreciated our candor and that we were advocating for them. They were happy we presented our findings without judgment or pressure and that we gave them a comprehensive written strategy that included actionable and measurable goals.

As a retirement planner—and not simply an accumulation advisor—that's my primary responsibility. As much as I love making people's days and lives by delivering good news, my job is to deliver good plans. That sometimes means being completely transparent and telling the truth, even when the truth stings.

****

It also means having a proven process that helps clients **connect**, **strategize**, and **plan**. Using the **Your Merkle Plan** process, we craft and deliver custom strategies designed to meet specific needs.

Your Merkle Plan

1) **Connect.** Our process starts with a simple fifteen-minute phone call where we get to know you and give you the chance to get to know us. We'll talk about your priorities, your concerns, your goals, and your current situation. At the end of the call, if we both decide to move forward, we'll schedule a Connection Visit.

   This Connection Visit helps us fully understand where you are now, and where you want to go. We want to see your retirement vision and understand how you plan to spend your retirement days. I'll discuss this in greater detail in the final chapter, but one of our top priorities is developing meaningful, lifelong relationships with our clients, as well as sound financial strategies. We want to connect with clients both inside *and* outside the walls of our firm because we're committed to building a community of people we care about, not just a customer base. If we want to continue after our Connection Visit, then we will schedule a Strategy Session.

2) **Strategize.** Developing strategies that maximize your retirement savings includes analyzing key aspects of your portfolio. We assess investment risk, fees, Social Security benefits, potential tax-saving strategies, long-term care risk, and more. We'll help you better understand your portfolio, showing you how we can add value and gain efficiencies. After we collaborate on how to effectively build **Your Merkle Plan**, we'll make a mutual decision about whether to continue planning your retirement together.

3) **Plan.** In this final stage, we work together on a strategy for each of the six components of retirement and incorporate them into **Your Merkle Plan**. The organization and transparency of this written plan can guide you confidently to and through retirement,

easing the anxiety you may have about this all-important transition. If your retirement vision or life circumstances change, your plan can easily be updated. That way, you can spend your time focusing on all the fun you will have in retirement. That's the true power of planning.

****

As a former baseball and football player at Central College in Pella, Iowa, I'm familiar with game plans. I remember the difference a key play call, substitution, or clutch performance can have. I know the benefits of leveraging strengths and limiting weaknesses. I understand the significance of research, analysis, and crystal-clear communication.

As important as those things are on the gridiron and ball diamond, they're even more essential in the world of retirement planning. I don't mean to sound overly dramatic, but without a solid financial game plan that addresses every aspect of your wealth, you could leave yourself susceptible to a costly error that could potentially jeopardize your future.

Retirement planning today is much more complex than it was for previous generations. I remember, for instance, how my grandfather retired in the mid-1980s with only a modest amount of savings, a pension, and Social Security. However, he and my grandmother enjoyed a wonderful retirement that included travel and many other great opportunities and adventures. Today, with pension scarcity, tax worries, rising health care costs, Social Security uncertainty, soaring inflation, and more, much of the onus is on you, the individual.

That means you need a holistic plan that will help you address a host of questions like these:

- Am I assuming an appropriate amount of investment risk to achieve my goals?
- Have I secured tax-efficient retirement withdrawal strategies and income streams?
- When is the optimal time *for me* to begin taking Social Security?

- Does my plan factor in that Americans, on average, are living longer lives?
- Will my family be well cared for, long after I'm gone?
- How can I afford the high cost of long-term care?

As you will see in the ensuing chapters, the point of this book is to help you begin finding answers to those questions and many more. My goal is to help you start drawing up a game plan of your own that accounts for numerous variables and conditions. Why? Because I'm convinced that the only thing standing between you and that dream trip, glorious vacation home, new hobby, or move to be near family and friends is a strategy tailored to your distinct needs and goals.

Your post-work years should be a time to relax. A time to make your mark and make a difference. A time to shed the old and embrace the new. This is a time to reflect on who you are, where you came from, and why you're here, so you can embark on adventures of the heart and retire your way!

Potential Risks to Your Ideal Retirement

Ever feel like life gets in the way and prevents you from doing things you should not ignore? I think if we're honest with ourselves, we've all put off obligations we know are important.

In your case, you may be reading this book because it's time to get serious about retirement planning and, specifically, devising a way to best prepare for retirement. A retirement plan should be based on more components than just your investments or your finances. The preparation of that strategy begins with your desires, ambitions, and goals for this fulfilling season of life.

There's no such thing as a silly question. Not when one of the most common questions we hear from folks regarding retirement is, "Am I going to be okay?" Often, it seems, people are reluctant to meet with financial professionals because they worry they might sound uneducated. Yet, it's understandable for you to be a novice when it comes to financial issues and retirement concerns. You've been busy with your lives and your careers. Time spent away from work has meant time spent being around those you love and engaging in the activities you enjoy. Retirement provides the opportunity to do even more of that, while not fretting over work obligations.

Concerns people have about what they may encounter during retirement can be far-reaching and still perfectly legitimate. For a quick snapshot, I want to provide a brief sampling of wide-ranging issues that can come up during discussions about what to potentially brace for in retirement. This book will touch on many of these issues in further detail.

Politics: A presidential election often stirs emotions regarding potential effects on the economy. Investors grow anxious about how a new president can influence market returns. It's Congress, however, that establishes tax laws and passes spending bills. Yet the president can indirectly affect the economy and the stock market in various ways such as the appointment of policymakers, development of international relations, and influential sway on new legislation.

Taxes: An example of a president's influence can be cited in signature legislation passed during Donald Trump's presidency, the Tax Cuts and Jobs Act of 2017. However, our tax system remains progressive, so the more you earn, the higher the tax rate within each tax bracket of subsequently higher income. A thorough understanding of tax regulations can be crucial. A retirement planner can help identify potential issues a tax professional can help solve.

Inflation: Government spending, which most recently spiked with relief packages designed to assist U.S. citizens during the COVID-19 pandemic, can fuel concerns of inflationary hikes stemming from an influx of money thrust at the same consumer goods. A retiree's income can be impacted by the effect inflation can have on a fixed budget. The value of currency decreases because inflation erodes purchasing power.

Health pandemic: The coronavirus outbreak could impact how Americans view risks and re-examine healthy habits. That, potentially, could be one of the effects of COVID-19 as we assess how long a pandemic can last and if others will occur in our lifetimes. The cost of health care can be surprising throughout retirement. It could become an issue people focus on even more following the pandemic, which had a particularly acute impact on some U.S. elder care facilities.

Cybersecurity: Think you'll give up your smartphone in retirement? No way, right? It's here to stay, along with other intellectual gadgetry, including devices that have not been patented or invented. Retirees are becoming more tech-savvy, yet they can also be more trusting, which can be problematic when responding to potential scammers by phone, text, or email. Cybercrime often uses technology to target potential victims. Scammers, much like technology, figure to only grow more sophisticated over time.

CHAPTER 1

Longevity

You would think the prospect of the grave would loom more frightening as we age, yet many retirees say their number one concern is actually running out of money in their twilight years.[1] This concern is, unfortunately, justified, in part, because of one significant factor: We're living longer.

According to the Social Security Administration's 2011 Trustee Report, in 1950, the average life expectancy for a sixty-five-year-old man was seventy-eight, and the average for a sixty-five-year-old woman was eighty-one. In the 2022 Trustees Report issued by the SSA, those averages were eighty-three and eighty-five, respectively.[2]

The bottom line of many retirees' budget woes comes down to this: They just didn't plan to live so long. Now, when we are younger and in our working years, that's not something we necessarily see as a bad thing; don't some people fantasize about living forever or, at least, reaching the ripe old age of one hundred?

However, with a longer lifespan, as we near retirement, we face a few snags. Our resources are finite—we only have so much money to provide income—but our lifespans can be

---

[1] Liz Weston. nerdwallet.com. March 25, 2021. "Will You Really Run Out of Money in Retirement?"
https://www.nerdwallet.com/article/finance/will-you-really-run-out-of-money-in-retirement
[2] Social Security Administration. 2022 Trustees Report. "Actuarial Life Table" https://www.ssa.gov/oact/STATS/table4c6.html

unpredictably long, perhaps longer than our resources allow. Also, longer lives don't necessarily equate with healthier lives. The longer you live, the more money you will likely need to spend on health care, even excluding long-term care needs like nursing homes.

You will also run into inflation. If you don't plan to live another twenty-five years but end up doing so, inflation at an average 3 percent will approximately double the price of goods over that time period. Put a harsh twist on that and the buying power of a ninety-year-old will be half of what they possessed if they retired at sixty-five.[3]

Because we don't necessarily get to have our cake and eat it, too, our collective increased longevity hasn't necessarily increased the healthy years of our lives. Typically, our life-extending care most widely applies to the time in our lives where we will need more care in general. Think of common situations like a pacemaker at eighty-five, or cancer treatment at seventy-eight.

"Wow, Loren," I can hear you say. "Way to start with the good news first."

I know, I've painted a grim picture, but all I'm concerned about here is cost. It's hard to put a dollar sign on life, but that is essentially what we're talking about when discussing longevity and finances. Living longer isn't a bad thing; it just costs more, and one key to a sound retirement strategy is preparing for it in advance.

Here's a story of one woman that illustrates this picture perfectly. Her mother passed away in her late seventies after years of suffering from Alzheimer's disease. Her father died at eighty from cancer. With modern medicine and treatment, this woman survived two rounds of breast cancer, lived with diabetes, and relied on a pacemaker, extending her life to age eighty-eight, nearly a decade beyond what she anticipated.

---

[3] Bob Sullivan, Benjamin Curry. Forbes. April 28, 2021. "Inflation And Retirement Investments: What You Need to Know."
https://www.forbes.com/advisor/retirement/inflation-retirement-investments/

However, she and her husband had saved and planned for "just in case," trying to be prepared if they had to move, needed nursing home care, or needed to help children and grandchildren with their expenses.

One of their "just-in-case" scenarios was living much longer than they anticipated. The last six years of her life were fraught with medical expenses, but she was also blessed with knowing her five great-grandchildren and deepening relationships with her children and grandchildren. She was able to pay for her own medical care, including her final two years in a nursing home, and her twilight years were truly golden.

From age eighty-five to eighty-eight, she was more socially active, with many visits from family and friends. She participated in more activities than she had in the seven years since her husband died. Her planning from decades earlier allowed her to pass on a legacy to her children when she passed away herself. The legacy she left behind can be measured both in dollar signs *and* in other intangible ways.

Living longer may be more expensive, but it can be so meaningful when you plan for your "just-in-cases."

Retiring Early

A key part of planning for retirement revolves around retirement income. After all, retirement is cutting the cord that tethers you to your employer—and your monthly check. However, that check often comes with many other benefits, particularly health care. Health care is often the thing that can unexpectedly put dreams for an early retirement on hold. Some employers offer health benefits to their retired workers, but that number has declined drastically over the past several decades. In 1988, among employers who offered health benefits to their workers, 66 percent offered health benefits to their retirees. In 2022, that number was 21 percent.[4]

---

4 Henry J. Kaiser Family Foundation. October 27, 2022. "2022 Employer Health Benefits Survey Section Eleven: Retiree Health Benefits."

So, with employer-offered retirement health benefits on the wane, this becomes a major point of concern for anyone who is looking to retire, particularly those who are looking to retire before age sixty-five, when they would become eligible for Medicare coverage. Fidelity estimates that the average retired couple at age sixty-five will need approximately $315,000 for health care expenses in retirement, not including long-term care.[5] Do you think it's likely that cost will decrease?

Even if you are working until age sixty-five or have plans to cover your health expenses until that point, I often have clients who incorrectly assume Medicare is their golden ticket to cover all expenses. That is simply not the case.

Retiring Later

Planning for a long life in retirement partly depends on when you retire. While many people end up retiring earlier than they anticipated—due to injuries, layoffs, family crises, and other unforeseen circumstances—continuing to work past age sixty (and even sixty-five) is still a viable option for others and can be an excellent way to help establish financial comfort in retirement.

There are many reasons for this. For one, you obviously still earn a paycheck and the benefits accompanying it. Medical coverage and beefing up your retirement accounts with further savings can be significant by themselves but continuing your income also should keep you from dipping into your retirement funds, further allowing them the opportunity to grow.

Additionally, for many workers, their nine-to-five job is more than just clocking in and out. Having a sense of purpose can keep us active physically, mentally, and socially. That kind

---

https://www.kff.org/report-section/ehbs-2022-section-11-retiree-health-benefits/

5 Fidelity Viewpoints. Fidelity. August 29, 2022.. "How to Plan for Rising Health Care Costs." https://www.fidelity.com/viewpoints/personal-finance/plan-for-rising-health-care-costs

of activity and level of engagement may also help stave off many of the health problems that plague retirees. Avoiding a sedentary life is one of the advantages of staying plugged into the workforce, if possible.

Consider, for instance, a couple I met about eight years ago—the husband was a professor at a local college, and the wife worked for a local financial company. While they were separated by only two months in age, their retirement visions were miles apart.

The wife couldn't wait to retire and start enjoying all the freedom of time and exploration that retirement can bring, but the husband wasn't nearly ready. He liked what he did and couldn't see himself giving it up—at least not yet.

She envisioned a retirement where they could travel, spend more time with the kids and grandkids, go on much longer bike rides, and really explore this new life together. In his mind, he was already retired. He was doing what he wanted when he wanted to do it. Yes, that included biking, hanging out with the family, and taking the occasional trip, but much of his fulfillment also came from his work and daily routine.

In addition to having different visions for the future, they weren't financially ready to retire. They were six figures in debt and didn't have nearly enough saved. Regardless of their wishes, they simply didn't have an immediate path forward to retirement, and this created real tension in their relationship.

We went to work on their plan, creating a debt repayment strategy that worked well with a retirement savings plan. We also created a retirement timeline that satisfied both.

Today, after years of diligently paying down their debt and committing to the savings plan, they are seventy-one, still working, and happy as can be. They now have very little debt, seven figures saved, and complete confidence in their financial direction. They also have a level of comfort they previously couldn't have imagined, and he now has a retirement target of seventy-five.

Over the course of this couple's eight-year journey, I saw how financial instability and uncertainty exacerbated tensions and complicated other decisions. The wife especially felt the stress of financial insecurity, which made everything else, including the pressures of her job, even more stressful.

But that was then. No longer burdened by the weight of financial struggles, she now has found she enjoys her work a great deal. Even though she could retire at any time, she isn't ready to give up that true source of fulfillment. She's approaching retirement her way, examining her career one year at a time. When the joy of work begins to fade, then—and only then—will she move on to her post-work chapter.

Health Care

Take a second to reflect on your health care plan. Although working up to or even past age sixty-five would allow you to avoid a coverage gap between your working years and Medicare, that may not be an option for you. Even if it is, when you retire, you will need to make some decisions about what kind of insurance coverage you may need to supplement your Medicare. Are there any medical needs you have that may require coverage in addition to Medicare? Did your parents or grandparents have any inherited medical conditions you might consider using a special savings plan to cover?

These are all questions that are important to review with your financial professional so you can be sure you have enough money put aside for health care.

Long-Term Care

Longevity means the need for long-term care is statistically more likely to happen. If you intend to pass on a legacy, planning for long-term care is paramount, since most estimates project nearly 70 percent of Americans will need some type of it.[6] However, this may be one of the biggest, most stressful pieces of longevity planning I encounter in my work. For one thing, who wants to talk about the point in their lives when they may feel the most limited? Who wants to dwell on what will happen if they no longer can toilet, bathe, dress, or feed themselves?

I get it; this is a less-than-fun part of planning. But a little bit of preparation now can go a long way!

When it comes to your longevity, just like with your goals, one of the important things to do is sit and dream. It may not be the fun, road-trip-to-the-Grand-Canyon kind of dreaming, but you can spend time envisioning how you want your twilight years to look.

For instance, if it is important for you to live in your home for as long as possible, who will provide for the day-to-day fixes and to-dos of housework if you become ill? Will you set aside money for a service, or do you have relatives or friends nearby whom you could comfortably allow to help you? Do you prefer in-home care over a nursing home or assisted living? This could be a good time to discuss the possibility of moving into a retirement community versus staying where you are or whether it's worth moving to another state and leaving relatives behind.

These are all important factors to discuss with your spouse and children, as *now* is the right time to address questions and concerns. For instance, is aging in place more important to one spouse than the other? Are the friends or relatives who live nearby emotionally, physically, and financially capable of helping you for a time if you face an illness?

Many families I meet with find these conversations very uncomfortable, particularly when children discuss nursing home care with their parents. A knee-jerk reaction for many is to promise they will care for their aging parents. This is noble

---

6 Richard W. Johnson. urban.org. June 24, 2021. "What is the Lifetime Risk of Needing and Receiving Long-Term Services and Supports?" https://www.urban.org/research/publication/what-lifetime-risk-needing-and-receiving-long-term-services-and-supports

and well-intentioned, but there needs to be an element of realism here. Does "help" from an adult child mean they stop by and help you with laundry, cooking, home maintenance, and bills? Or does it mean they move you into their spare room when you have hip surgery? Are they prepared to help you use the restroom and bathe if that becomes difficult for you to do on your own?

I don't mean to discourage families from caring for their own; this can be a profoundly admirable relationship when it works out. However, I've seen families put off planning for late-in-life care based on a tenuous promise that the adult children would care for their parents, only to watch as the support system crumbles. Sometimes this is because the assumed caregiver hasn't given serious thought to the preparation they would need, both in a formal sense and regarding their personal physical, emotional, and financial commitments. This is often also because we can't see the future: Alzheimer's disease and other maladies of old age can exact a heavy toll. When a loved one reaches the point where he or she is at risk of wandering away or needs help with two or more activities of daily living, it can be more than one person or family can realistically handle.

If you know what you want, communicate with your family about both the best-case and worst-case scenarios. Then, hope for the best, and plan for the worst.

Realistic Cost of Care

Wrapped up in your planning should be a consideration for the cost of long-term care. The potential costs for such care and treatment can be underestimated, especially by those who have maintained robust health and find it difficult to envision future declines to their condition.

Another piece of planning for long-term care costs is anticipating inflation. It's common knowledge that prices have been and keep rising, which will lower your purchasing power on everything from food to medical care. Long-term care is a big piece of the inflation-disparity pie.

While local costs vary from state to state, following is the national median for various forms of long-term care (plus projections that account for a 3 percent annual inflation, so you can see what I am referencing):[7]

Long-Term Care Costs: Inflation				
	Home Health Care, Homemaker Services	Adult Day Care	Assisted Living	Nursing Home (semi-private room)
Annual 2021	$59,488	$20,280	$54,000	$94,900
Annual 2031	$79,947	$27,255	$72,571	$127,538
Annual 2041	$107,442	$36,628	$97,530	$171,400
Annual 2051	$144,393	$49,225	$131,072	$230,347

Fund Your Long-Term Care

One critical mistake I see are those who haven't planned for long-term care because they assume the government will provide everything. But that's a big misconception. The government has two health insurance programs: Medicare and Medicaid. These can greatly assist you in your health care needs in retirement but usually don't provide enough coverage to cover all your health care costs in retirement. I'm going to give an overview of both, but if you want to dive into the details of

---

7 Genworth Financial. June 2022. "Cost of Care Survey 2022."
https://www.genworth.com/aging-and-you/finances/cost-of-care.html

these programs, you can visit www.Medicare.gov and www.Medicaid.gov.

Medicare

Medicare covers those aged sixty-five and older and those who are disabled. Medicare's coverage of any nursing-home-related health issues is limited. It might cover your nursing home stay if it is not a "custodial" stay, and it isn't long-term. For example, if you break a bone or suffer a stroke, stay in a nursing home for rehabilitative care, and then return home, Medicare may cover you. But, if you have developed dementia or are looking to move to a nursing facility because you can no longer bathe, dress, toilet, feed yourself, or take care of your hygiene, etc., then Medicare is not going to pay for your nursing home costs.[8]

You can enroll in Medicare anytime during the three months before and three months after your sixty-fifth birthday. Miss your enrollment deadline, and you could risk paying increased premiums for the rest of your life.[9] On top of prompt enrollment, there are a few other things to think about when it comes to Medicare, not least among them being the need to understand the different "parts," what they do, and what they don't cover.

Part A

Medicare Part A is what you might think of as "classic" Medicare. Hospital care, some types of home health care, and major medical care fall under this. While most enrollees pay nothing for this service (as they likely paid into the system for at least ten years), you may end up paying, either based on work history or delayed signup. In 2023, the highest premium is

---

[8] Medicare.gov. "What Part A covers." https://www.medicare.gov/what-medicare-covers/part-a/what-part-a-covers.html

[9] Medicare.gov. "When can I sign up for Medicare?" https://www.medicare.gov/basics/get-started-with-medicare/sign-up/when-can-i-sign-up-for-medicare

$506 per month, and a hospital stay does have a deductible, $1,600.[10] And, if you have a hospital stay that surpasses sixty days, you could be looking at additional costs; keep in mind, Medicare doesn't pay for long-term care and services.

Part B

Medicare Part B is an essential piece of wrap-around coverage for Medicare Part A. It helps pay for doctor visits and outpatient services. This also comes with a price tag: Although the Part B deductible is only $226 in 2023, you will still pay 20 percent of all costs after that, with no limit on out-of-pocket expenses. The Part B monthly premium for 2023 ranges from the standard amount of $164.90 to $560.50.[11]

Part C

Medicare Part C, more commonly known as Medicare Advantage plans, are an alternative to a combination of Parts A, B, and sometimes D. Administered through private insurance companies, these have a variety of costs and restrictions, and they are subject to the specific policies and rules of the issuing carrier.

Part D

Medicare Part D is also through a private insurer and is supplemental to Parts A and B, as its primary purpose is to cover prescription drugs. Like any private insurance plan, Part D has its quirks and rules that vary from insurer to insurer.

---

[10] Medicare. "Medicare 2023 Costs at a Glance."
https://www.medicare.gov/your-medicare-costs/medicare-costs-at-a-glance
[11] Ibid.

The Donut Hole

Even with a "Part D" in place, you may still have a coverage gap between what your Part D private drug insurance pays for your prescription and what basic Medicare pays. In 2023, the coverage gap is $4,660, meaning, after you meet your private prescription insurance limit, you will spend no more than 25 percent of your drug costs out-of-pocket before Medicare will kick in to pay for more prescription drugs.[12]

Medicare Supplements

Medicare Supplement Insurance, MedSupp, Medigap, or plans labeled Medicare Part F, G, H, I, J . . . Known by a variety of monikers, this is just a fancy way of saying "medical coverage for those over sixty-five that picks up the tab for whatever the federal Medicare program(s) doesn't." Again, costs, limitations, etc., vary by carrier.

Does that sound like a bunch of government alphabet soup to you? It certainly does to me. And, did you read the fine print? Unpredictable costs, varied restrictions, difficult-to-compare benefits, donut holes, and coverage gaps. That's par for the course with health care plans through the course of our adult lives. What gives? I thought Medicare was supposed to be easier, comprehensive, and at no cost!

The truth is there is probably no stage of life when health care is easy to understand.

If you think Social Security, with up to eighty-one options, is complex, try wading or weeding through your Medicare choices. Chances are you'll be completely overwhelmed.

With Social Security, once you make your benefits election, rarely will you have to worry about changing it. With Medicare, you must decide each year if you want to stay the course or take a different route. You must decipher whether original Medicare

---

[12] Medicare. "Costs in the coverage gap." https://www.medicare.gov/drug-coverage-part-d/costs-for-medicare-drug-coverage/costs-in-the-coverage-gap

and its Medigap alphabet are best for you, or if you'd be better off with one of those Medicare Advantage plans you hear about in all the commercials.

Most retirement health care studies say a retired couple who is sixty-five will pay $315,000 in health care costs alone over the course of their retirement, and this doesn't include the cost of long-term care. So, the pressure to get this decision right—not only once, but again and again every year—is daunting. Couple the complexity of the myriad options with consistently changing legislation, and it's enough to make one think of Medicare as an impossible mission.

It really isn't, though. We have a Medicare specialist as a part of our team who focuses solely on health care and Medicare planning for our families. She works directly with our retirement planners to make sure the elements of their retirement plans, like our tax strategies, work with the Medicare decisions. The choices our families make with their tax plan can have a direct impact on their cost of Medicare. If this nuance is missed, it can cause a significant increase in their already-expensive Medicare coverage.

The best thing you can do for yourself is to scope out the health care field early, compare costs often, and prepare for out-of-pocket costs well in advance—decades, if possible.

Medicaid

Medicaid is a program the states administer, so funding, protocol, and limitations vary. Compared to Medicare, Medicaid more widely covers nursing home care, but it targets a different demographic: those with low incomes.

If you have more assets than the Medicaid limit in your state and need nursing home care, you will need to use those assets to pay for your care. You will also have a list of additional state-approved ways to spend some of these assets over the Medicaid limit, such as pre-purchasing burial plots and funeral expenses or paying off debts. After that, your remaining assets fund your nursing home stay until they are gone, at which point Medicaid will jump in.

Some people aren't stymied by this, thinking they will just pass on their financial assets early, gifting them to relatives, friends, and causes so they can qualify for Medicaid when they need it. However, to prevent this exact scenario, Uncle Sam has implemented the look-back period. Currently, if you enroll in Medicaid, you are subject to having the government scrutinize the last five years of your finances for large gifts or expenses that may subject you to penalties, temporarily making you ineligible for Medicaid coverage.

So, if you're planning to preserve your money for future generations and retain control of your financial resources during your lifetime, you'll probably want to prepare for the costs of longevity beyond a "government plan."

Self-Funding

One way to fund a longer life is the old-fashioned way, through self-funding. There are a variety of financial tools you can use, and they all have their pros and cons. If your assets are in low-interest financial vehicles (savings, bonds, CDs), you risk letting inflation erode the value of your dollar. Or, if you are relying on the stock market, you have more growth potential, but you'll also want to consider the possible implications of market volatility. What if your assets take a hit? If you suffer a loss in your retirement portfolio in early or mid-retirement, you might have the option to "tighten your belt," so to speak, and cut back on discretionary spending to allow your portfolio the room to bounce back. But, if you are retired and depend on income from a stock account that just hit a downward stride, what are you going to do?

HSAs

These days, you might also be able to self-fund through a health savings account, or HSA, if you have access to one through a high-deductible health plan (you will not qualify to save in an HSA after enrolling in Medicare). In an HSA, any growth of your tax-deductible contributions will be tax-free, and any distributions paid out for qualified health costs are also tax-free. Long-term care expenses count as health costs, so, if this is an option available to you, it is one way to use the tax advantages to self-fund your longevity. Bear in mind, if you are younger than sixty-five, any money you use for nonqualified expenses will be subject to taxes and penalties, and, if you are older than sixty-five, any HSA money you use for non-medical expenses is subject to income tax.

LTCI

One slightly more nuanced way to pay for longevity, specifically for long-term care, is long-term care insurance, or LTCI. As car insurance protects your assets in case of a car accident and home insurance protects your assets in case something happens to your house, long-term care insurance aims to protect your assets in case you need long-term care in an at-home or nursing home situation.

As with other types of insurance, you will pay a monthly or annual premium in exchange for an insurance company paying for long-term care down the road. Typically, policies cover two to three years of care, which is adequate for an "average" situation: it's estimated 70 percent of Americans will need about three years of long-term care of some kind.

Now, there are a few oft-cited components of LTCI that make it unattractive for some:

- Expense — LTCI can be expensive. It is generally less expensive the younger you are, but a sixty-five-year-old couple who purchased LTCI in 2022 could expect to pay a combined amount of $3,750 each year for an average three-year coverage policy. And the annual cost only increases from there the older you are.[13]

---

[13] American Association for Long-Term Care Insurance. 2023. . "Long-Term Care Insurance Facts – Data – Statistics – 2022 Reports" https://www.aaltci.org/long-term-care-insurance/learning-center/ltcfacts-2022.php#2022costs-65

- Limited options — Let's face it: LTCI may be expensive for consumers, but it can also be expensive for companies that offer it. With fewer companies willing to take on that expense, this narrows the market, meaning opportunities to price shop for policies with different options or custom benefits are limited.

- If you know you need it, you might not be able to get it — Insurance companies offering LTCI are taking on a risk that you may need LTCI. That risk is the foundation of the product—you may or may not need it. If you know you will need it because you have a dementia diagnosis or another illness for which you will need long-term care, you will likely not qualify for LTCI coverage.

- Use it or lose it—If you have LTCI and are in the minority of Americans who die having never needed long-term care, all the money you paid into your LTCI policy is gone.

- Possibly fluctuating rates—Your rate is not locked in on LTCI. Companies maintain the ability to raise or lower your premium amounts. This means some seniors face an ultimatum: Keep funding a policy at what might be a less affordable rate *or* lose coverage and let go of all the money they paid in so far.

After that, you might be thinking, "How can people possibly be interested in LTCI?" But let me repeat myself—as many as 70 percent of Americans will need long-term care. And, although only one in ten Americans age fifty-five-plus have purchased LTCI, keep in mind the high cost of nursing home care. Can you afford $7,000 a month to put into nursing home care and still have enough left over to protect your legacy? This is a very real concern considering one set of statistics reported a two-in-three chance that a senior citizen will become physically or cognitively impaired in their lifetime.[14] So, not to sound like a broken record, but it is vitally important to have a plan in place to deal with longevity and long-term care if you intend to leave a financial legacy.

At Merkle Retirement Planning, we don't typically recommend traditional LTCI, but we do work with the families we serve to build a long-term care plan. We do that by first determining a client's long-term care risk, then figuring out how to cover that risk. There are four primary ways or combinations of strategies to do so:

- Self-insure
- Traditional LTCI
- Hybrid LTCI/life insurance policy
- Income annuity with home health care benefits

Many people will choose not to buy traditional LTCI policies because they have changed a lot over the last twenty years and are not as attractive as they used to be. Because some question whether they'll need LTCI, they simply want to make sure the cost of LTCI doesn't disrupt their retirement plan. Using traditional LTCI, you could invest tens of thousands of dollars over the course of your retirement and never get a penny out of it. The good news is you didn't need LTCI; the bad news is you made a considerable investment with only comfort as your return.

Also, many LTCI companies have increased their premiums substantially. I've had multiple families come to me with rate increases from their LTCI companies, and it tells them that the rates will increase each year by about 30 percent annually for the next three years. They can accept the rate increases, accept a lower amount of coverage, or let it lapse. All the while, individuals are thinking in the back of their minds, "We may not ever even use this." The bottom line is traditional LTCI can create a dilemma that most retirees don't want or need.

---

[14] payingforseniorcare.com. 2022. "Long-Term Senior Care Statistics" https://www.payingforseniorcare.com/statistics

Hybrid LTCI/life insurance puts certainty into an otherwise uncertain world. With HLTCI, the premiums are locked in; they can never increase as long as you continue to pay. With many policies, you can choose to pay over a relatively short period of time, such as five or ten years. If you never need LTCI, then your beneficiaries receive a tax-free death benefit when you pass.

There are many variations to these polices, but here's a quick example that will give you an idea of how they work: Let's say you purchase a policy with a $200,000 death benefit. If you never need LTCI, when you pass away, your beneficiaries will receive $200,000 tax-free. If you need LTCI, then you advance the death benefit to pay for the LTCI expenses. The policy might allow you to advance 20 percent of the death benefit each year for five years—$40,000 per year for five years in this example. For most people, $40,000 isn't going to pay for all of their LTCI expenses, but it would offset some of the costs.

If you want to offset more of the risk, you simply purchase a bigger death benefit. If you purchased a $1 million policy, for instance, then you could offset $200,000 per year of your LTCI risk.

With this strategy, you have more control over how to cover your LTCI risk than with traditional LTCI. You are more certain of what your lifetime investment will be, as well.

A few relevant statistics to keep in mind:

- The longer you live, the more likely you are to continue living; the longer you live, the more health care you will likely need to pay for.
- The average cost of a private nursing home room in the United States in 2021 was $9,034 a month.[15] But keep in mind, that is just the nursing home—it doesn't include other medical costs, let alone pleasantries, like entertainment or hobby spending.

---

[15] Genworth Financial. January 31, 2022. "Genworth 2020 Cost of Care Survey." https://www.genworth.com/aging-and-you/finances/cost-of-care.html

- In 2022, Fidelity calculated that a healthy couple retiring at age sixty-five could expect to pay around $315,000 over the course of retirement to cover health and medical expenses.

I know. Whoa, there, Loren, I was hoping to have a realistic idea of health costs, not be driven over by a cement mixer!

The good news is, while we don't know these exact costs in advance, we know there *will* be costs. And you won't have to pay your total Medicare lifetime premiums in one day as a lump sum. Now that you have a good idea of health care costs in retirement, you can *plan* for them! That's the real point, here: Planning in advance can keep you from feeling nickel-and-dimed to your wits' end. Instead, having a sizeable portion of your assets earmarked for health care can allow you the freedom to choose health care networks, coverage options, and long-term care possibilities you like and that you think offer you the best in life.

Product Riders

LTCI and self-funding are not the only ways to plan for the expenses of longevity. Some companies are getting creative with their products, particularly insurance companies. One way they are retooling to meet people's needs is through optional product riders on annuities and life insurance. Elsewhere in this book, I talk about annuity basics, but here's a brief overview: Annuities are insurance contracts. You pay the insurance company a premium, either as a lump sum or as a series of payments over a set amount of time, in exchange for guaranteed income payments. One of the advantages of an annuity is it has access to riders, which allow you to tweak your contract for a fee, usually about 1 percent of the contract value annually. One annuity rider some companies offer is a long-term care rider. If you have an annuity with a long-term care rider and are not in need of long-term care, your contract behaves as any annuity contract would—nothing changes. Generally speaking, if you reach a point when you can't perform multiple functions of daily life on your own, you notify the insurance company, and a representative will turn on those provisions of your contract.

Like LTCI, different companies and products offer different options. Some annuity long-term care riders offer coverage of two years in a nursing home situation. Others cap expenses at two times the original annuity's value. It greatly depends. Some people prefer this option because there isn't a "use-it-or-lose-it" piece; if you die without ever having needed long-term care, you still will have had the income benefit from the base contract. Still, as with any annuities or insurance contracts, there are the usual restrictions and limitations. Withdrawing money from the contract will affect future income payments, early distributions can result in a penalty, income taxes may apply, and, because the insurance company's solvency is what guarantees your payments, it's important to do your research about the insurance company you are considering purchasing a contract from.

Understandably, a discussion on long-term care is bound to feel at least a little tedious. Yet, this is a critical piece of planning for income in retirement, particularly if you want to leave a legacy.

A while back, we received a call from an individual who had been watching our weekly, thirty-minute TV show. The man explained that he was concerned about long-term care because he had witnessed both ends of the planning spectrum with his divorced parents.

His mom, he said, planned well for LTCI. Good thing, too, because she needed it for four years. Because her coverage was sound, she was able to afford quality care and was treated well. She also passed on a considerable amount of money upon her death, despite paying for years of care.

His dad, on the other hand, already has exhausted his financial resources after two years of care, the son said. Now on Medicaid, he isn't doing well.

Witnessing these two vastly different experiences firsthand inspired this gentleman to start planning like his mother. He's determined to make sure his wife will be able to live a comfortable retirement, even if he someday requires care. He's equally determined to pass on a financial legacy to his children if one or both parents need assistance.

Spousal Planning

Here's one thing to keep in mind no matter how you plan to save: Many of us will be planning for more than ourselves. Look back at all the stats on health events and the likelihood of long life and long-term care. If they hold true for a single individual, then the likelihood of having a costly health or long-term care event is even higher for a married couple. You'll be planning for not just one life, but two. So, when it comes to long-term care insurance, annuities, self-funding, or whatever strategy you are looking at using, be sure you are funding longevity for the both of you.

CHAPTER 2

Taxes

Where to begin with taxes? Perhaps by acknowledging we all bear responsibility for the resources we share. Roads, bridges, schools . . . it is the patriotic duty of every American to pay their fair share of taxes. Many would agree with me. However, while they don't mind paying their fair share, they're not interested in paying one cent more than that!

Now, just talking taxes probably takes your mind to April—tax season. You are probably thinking about all the forms you collect and how you file. Perhaps you are thinking about your certified public accountant or another qualified tax professional and saying to yourself, "I've already got taxes taken care of, thanks!"

However, what I see when people come into my office is that their relationship with their tax professional is purely a January through April relationship. That means they may have a tax professional, but not a tax *planner*.

What I mean is tax planning extends beyond filing taxes. In April, we are required to settle our accounts with the IRS to make sure we have paid up on our bill or to even the score if we have overpaid. But real tax planning is about making each financial move in a way that allows you to keep the most money in your pocket to use towards your retirement lifestyle.

Now, as a caveat, I want to emphasize I am not a CPA, but I see the way taxes affect my clients, and I have plenty of experience helping clients implement tax-efficient strategies in their retirement plans in conjunction with their tax professionals.

With the families we serve, we can work with their CPA to help them implement a tax plan. We do this because most CPAs don't consider a client's next ten, twenty, or thirty years. They simply look at what happened the previous year and possibly at what might take place in the current year. That's about it.

Not long ago, I had someone—I'll call him Ed—come visit me about a week after he attended one of our live workshops. "You know, you were right," Ed told me.

"About what?" I asked.

Ed proceeded to tell me that, after the workshop, he went to his advisor, told him about the workshop discussion, and asked the advisor if he could incorporate similar tax strategies into his plan. "We don't do that," the advisor explained. "You need to, talk to your CPA."

Ed then visited his CPA, only to hear him say something similar and refer him to a retirement planner.

CPAs, you see, are trained to try and decrease your tax liability for the previous year. That's partly why you hire them, because you don't want to pay more than you need to during a given year.

However, some of the most effective long-term tax-planning strategies require you to pay more in taxes sooner rather than later. Yes, I said that correctly. Some of the most effective ways to decrease your retirement tax bill is to intentionally pay more in tax *now* than what is required!

It is especially important to me to help my clients develop tax-efficient strategies in their retirement plans. Each dollar they can keep in their pockets is a dollar they can use toward their lifestyle or legacy plans.

Everyone has a retirement tax bill. Most baby boomers have the majority of their retirement savings in pre-tax accounts such as 401(k) plans or IRAs. These accounts contain money that has grown tax-deferred over the years.

So, when that money is withdrawn during retirement, retirees must pay taxes on it at whatever the ordinary tax rate is at the time. And here's the thing about tax rates: They have a habit of changing.

Sometimes at our workshops or on our TV show, I will say, "Taxes are on sale." When I say that, I sometimes get funny looks, because many people feel like they're currently paying a lot in taxes—and they probably are.

But when it comes to the tax rates, they're actually at historical lows. Right now, the lowest tax rate available to us is 10 percent. Prior to 2002, we have to go all the way back to 1941 to find another rate as low as 10 percent. The highest rate available to us right now is 37 percent. In 1980, that percentage was 70. The highest rate we have ever seen is 94 percent.

So, your tax bill might seem painful now, but history says it can get worse, especially if all or most of your retirement nest egg is in tax-deferred accounts—or accounts that will require taxes to be paid. Couple today's historically low rates with the fact that our national debt and deficit have never been higher, and it seems quite probable that these low tax rates will be temporary.

The Fed

Now, in the United States, taxes can be a rather uncertain proposition. Depending on who is in the White House and which party controls Congress, we might be tempted to assume tax rates could either decline or increase in the next four to eight years accordingly. However, there is one (large!) factor we, as a nation, must confront: the national debt.

Currently, according to USDebtClock.org, we are over $31,000,000,000,000 in debt and climbing. That's $31 *trillion* with a "T." With just $1 trillion, you could park it in the bank at a zero percent interest rate and spend more than $54 million every day for fifty years without hitting a zero balance.

Even if Congress got a handle and stopped that debt from its daily compound, divided by each taxpayer, we each would owe about $246,000. So, will that be check, cash, or Venmo?[16]

My point here isn't to give you anxiety. I'm just cautioning you that even with the rosiest of outlooks on our personal income tax rates, none of us should count on low tax rates for the long term. Instead, you and your network of professionals (tax, legal, and financial) should constantly be looking for ways to take advantage of tax-saving opportunities as they come. After all, the best "luck" is when proper planning meets opportunity.

So, how can we get started?

Know Your Limits

One of the foundational pieces of tax planning is knowing what tax bracket you are in, based on your income after subtracting pre-tax or untaxed assets. Your income taxes are based on your taxable income.

One reason to know your taxable income and your income tax rate is so you can see how far away you are from the next lower or higher tax bracket. This is particularly important when it comes to decisions such as gifting and Roth IRA conversions.

For instance, when confronting the 2022 federal income tax return they filed in 2023, Mallory and Ralph's taxable income is just over $345,000, putting them in the 32 percent tax bracket and about $4,900 above the upper end of the 24 percent tax bracket. They have already maxed out their retirement funds' tax-exempt contributions for the year. Their daughter, Gloria, is a sophomore in college. This couple could shave a considerable amount off their tax bill if they use the $4,900 to help Gloria out with groceries and school— something they were likely to do, anyway, but now can deliberately be put to work for them in their overall financial strategy.

---

[16] usdebtclock.org.

Now, I use Mallory and Ralph only as an example—your circumstances are probably different—but I think this nicely illustrates the way planning ahead for taxes can save you money.

Assuming a Lower Tax Rate

Many people anticipate being in a lower tax bracket in retirement. It makes sense: You won't be contributing to retirement funds; you'll be drawing from them. And you won't have all those work expenses—work clothes, transportation, lunch meetings, etc.

Yet, do you really plan on changing your lifestyle after retirement? Do you plan to reduce the number of times you eat out, scale back vacations, and skimp on travel?

What I see with the families and individuals that I serve is many couples spend more in the first few years, or maybe the first decade, of retirement. Sure, that may taper off later on, but usually only just in time for their budget to be hit with greater health and long-term care expenses.

Do you see where this is going? Many people plan as though their taxable income will be lower in retirement and are surprised when the tax bills come in and look more or less the same as they used to. It's better to plan for the worst and hope for the best, wouldn't you agree?

401(k)/IRA

One sometimes-unexpected piece of tax planning in retirement concerns your 401(k) or IRA. Most of us have one of these accounts or an equivalent. Throughout our working lives, we pay in, dutifully socking away a portion of our earnings in these tax-deferred accounts. There's the rub: tax-deferred. Not tax-free. Very rarely is anything free of taxation when you get down to it. Using 401(k)s and IRAs in retirement is no different. The taxes the government deferred when you were in your working years are now coming due, and you will pay taxes on that income at whatever your current tax rate is.

Just to ensure the IRS gets its due, the government also has a required minimum distribution, or RMD, rule. Beginning at age seventy-three, you are required to withdraw a certain minimum amount every year from your 401(k) or IRA, or else you will face a tax penalty on any RMD monies you should have withdrawn but didn't—and that's on top of income tax. The SECURE Act 2.0 reduced the penalty to 25 percent (from 50 percent). Timely corrections also can reduce the penalty to 10 percent.[17]

Of course, there is also the Roth account. You can think of the difference between a Roth and a traditional retirement account as the difference between taxing the seed and taxing the harvest. Because Roths are funded with post-tax dollars, there aren't tax penalties for early withdrawals of the principal nor are there taxes on the growth after you reach age fifty-nine-and-one-half. Perhaps best of all, there are no RMDs. Of course, you must own a Roth account for a minimum of five years before you are able to take advantage of all its features.

This is one more area where it pays to be aware of your tax bracket. Some people may find it advantageous to "convert" their traditional retirement account funds to Roth account funds in a year during which they are in a lower tax bracket. Others may opt to put any excess RMDs from their traditional retirement accounts into other products, like stocks or insurance.

Does that make your head spin? Understandable. That's why it's so important to work with a financial professional and tax planner who can help you execute these sorts of tax-efficient strategies and help you understand what you are doing and why.

There is a phenomenon that can happen in retirement that we call the tax ticking time bomb. It's that time in retirees' early

---

[17] Jim Probasco. Investopedia.com. January 6, 2023. "SECURE 2.0 Act of 2022." https://www.investopedia.com/secure-2-0-definition-5225115

seventies when they must begin taking RMDs and they have already turned on lifetime income streams such as Social Security and pensions (if they're among the lucky few to still receive pensions).

What happens is this: When permanent and taxable income is coupled with taxable RMD income, many retirees are pushed into an uncomfortably high tax bracket. Even worse, much of the time this tax rate comes as a complete surprise because they're making more than they ever imagined possible. Once they hit RMD age and are forced to take the excess income, boom! The tax ticking time bomb explodes, making the IRS the biggest benefactor.

The bottom line is everyone should have an intentional, custom tax plan. The most effective tax-planning strategies must be executed within the calendar year. You can't wait until April of the following tax year as you do with IRA contributions. That's why every December 31 that passes without implementation of forward-thinking tax planning is another year of potential opportunity missed.

CHAPTER 3

Market Volatility

U p and down. Roller coaster. Merry-go-round. Bulls and bears. Peak-to-trough.

Sound familiar? This is the language we use to talk about the stock market. With volatility and spikes, even our language is jarring, bracing, and vivid.

Still, financial strategies tend to revolve around market-based products, for good reasons. For one thing, there is no other financial class that packs the same potential for growth, pound for pound, as stock-based products. Because of growth potential, inflation protection, and new opportunities, it may be unwise to avoid the market entirely.

However, along with the potential for growth is the potential for loss. At the time this book was written, many of the people I've seen in my office came in feeling uneasy because of the economic fallout of the COVID-19 outbreak of 2020, followed by the economic downturn, and the inflation spike that happened in 2022.

So how do we balance these factors? How do we try to satisfy both the need for protection and the need for growth?

For one thing, it is important to recognize the value of diversity. Now, I'm not just talking about the diversity of assets among different kinds of stocks, or even different kinds of stocks and bonds. That's only one kind of diversity; while important, both stocks and bonds, though different, are both still market-based products. Most market-based products, even within a diverse portfolio, tend to rise or lower as a whole, just like an incoming tide. Take 2008 and 2022 as recent examples. Therefore, a portfolio diverse in only market-sourced products won't automatically protect your assets during times when the market declines.

In addition to the sort of "horizontal diversity" you have by purchasing a variety of stocks and bonds from different companies, I also suggest you think about "vertical diversity," or diversity among asset classes. This means having different product types, including securities products, bank products, and insurance products—with varying levels of growth potential, liquidity, and protection—all in accordance with your unique situation, goals, and needs.

Also, investors need to have a clear working knowledge of how much risk is in their portfolio. Meaning when the market goes through a bad cycle (on average, we go through a bear market every two to three years), you need to understand how much your portfolio can lose.

Both advisors and clients often get into trouble with market risk when they fail to clarify portfolio expectations. What I mean is most people talk about their capacity for market risk in very subjective terms. For instance, when I ask someone for the first time how they feel about market risk, I often will hear, "I'm conservative." Or "I want to be aggressive." Or "I'm just middle of the road."

The problem with those terms is they have different meanings to different people. If I'm working with a married couple, conservative might mean something different to one spouse than it does to the other. Or, even if they are on the same page, it might mean something different to me.

Most people only become concerned about risk when the markets are performing poorly. For example, if a couple has $1 million invested, and the market has dropped so much that their portfolio is down $150,000, the couple might go to their advisor and say, "What are you doing? We told you we wanted to be conservative."

However, the advisor is thinking, "What do you mean? The market is down 30 percent, and you are only down 15 percent. That is conservative."

Lack of clear expectations is the number one reason for poor investor decisions. That's why I talk about market risk with very clear language. It also is why I use technology to analyze a portfolio and get a good feel for how the portfolio is likely to react if it's invested in a particular way and we encounter a poor market cycle. I communicate that information clearly, too. For instance:

Mr. and Mrs. Jones, the way you currently have your portfolio invested, if we go through a really bad twelve months in the market, I would anticipate your $1 million portfolio losing $150,000. How does that make you feel?

Obviously, no one likes losing money, but it's imperative to clearly explain that their portfolio probably will be down if they invest in market-driven products and the market tumbles. The only real questions are: How big a hit will they take, and are they comfortable with it?

Once I've determined that, the conversation can continue:

If this is uncomfortable, then let's switch your plan so you don't go through that. Or, if you are comfortable with that, just be aware that your portfolio can move quite a bit.

This type of clear communication can minimize investor surprise and anxiety.

The Color of Money

When you're looking at the overall diversity of your portfolio, part of the equation is knowing which products fit in what category: what has liquidity, what has protection, and what has growth potential.

Before we dive in, keep in mind these aren't absolutes. You might think of liquidity, growth, and protection as primary colors. While some products will look pretty much yellow, red, or blue, others will have a mix of characteristics, making them more green, orange, or purple.

Growth

I like to think of the growth category as red. It's powerful, it's somewhat volatile, and it's also the category where we have the greatest opportunities for growth and loss. Often, products in the growth category will have a good deal of liquidity but very little protection. These are our market-based products and strategies, and we think of them mostly in shades of red and orange, to designate their growth and liquidity. This is a good place to be when you're young—think fast cars and flashy leather jackets—but its allure often wanes as you move closer to retirement. Examples of "red" products include:

- Stocks
- Equities
- Exchange-traded funds
- Mutual funds
- Corporate bonds
- Real estate investment trusts
- Speculations
- Alternative investments

Liquidity

Yellow is my liquid category color. I typically recommend having at least enough yellow money to cover six months' to a year's worth of expenses in case of emergency. Yellow assets don't need a lot of growth potential; they just need to be readily available when we need them. The "yellow" category includes assets like:

- Cash
- Money market accounts

Protection

The color of protection, to me, is blue. Tranquil, peaceful, sure, even if it lacks a certain amount of flash. This is the direction I like to see people generally move toward as they're nearing retirement. The red, flashy look of stock market returns and the risk of possible overnight losses is less attractive as we near retirement and look for more consistency and reliability. While this category doesn't come with a lot of liquidity, the products here are backed by an insurance company, a bank, or a government entity. "Blue" products include things such as:

- Certificates of deposit (backed by banks)
- Government-based bonds (backed by the U.S. government)
- Life insurance (backed by insurance companies)
- Annuities (backed by insurance companies)

For most people, market-based products are a reliable, long-term part of a diversified portfolio. If allocated appropriately, they can help retirees keep pace with inflation and protect against the possibility of rising taxes while not causing too much anxiety or fear when market volatility strikes.

While no one can control the markets, we can, to a large degree, control how portfolios react to them. On average, we see a recession every five to six years, so we should not be surprised by recessions, or bear markets, or even market corrections. They are all a regular part of investing. We just need to be prepared for them and make sure they don't keep you from retiring your way.

401(k)s

I want to take a second to specifically address a product many retirees will be using to build their retirement income: the 401(k) and other retirement accounts. Any of these retirement accounts (IRAs, 401(k)s, 403(b)s, etc.) are basically "tax wrappers." What do I mean by that? Well, depending on your plan provider, a 401(k) could include target-date funds, passively managed products, stocks, bonds, mutual funds, or even variable, fixed, and fixed index annuities, all collected in one place and governed by rules (a.k.a. the "tax wrapper"). These rules govern how much money you can put inside, what ways you can put it in, when you will pay taxes on it, and when you can take the money out. Inside the 401(k), each of the products inside the "tax wrapper" might have its own fees or commissions, in addition to the management fee you pay on the 401(k) itself.

Now, fees can be troublesome. You can't get something for nothing, and fees are how many financial companies and professionals make a living. Yet, it's important to recognize even a fee with a fraction of a percentage point is money out of your pocket—money that represents not just the one-time fee of today but also represents an opportunity cost. A $100,000 IRA that earns 6 percent over a twenty-five-year period without investment fees would earn $430,000. But if just a 0.5 percent fee got factored into that investment, the IRA would be worth $379,000 in twenty-five years, a $50,500 decrease.[18] For someone close to retirement, how much do you think fees may have cost over their lifetime?

Even for those close to retirement, it's important to look at management fees and assess if you think you're getting what you pay for. Over the course of ten years, those costs can add up, and you may have decades ahead of you in which you will need to rely on your assets.

Dollar-Cost Averaging

With 401(k)s and other market-based retirement products, dollar-cost averaging is a concept that can work in your favor

---

[18] Pam Krueger. Kiplinger.com. January 8, 2021. "How to Spot (and Squash) Nasty Fees That Hide in Your Investments" https://www.kiplinger.com/retirement/retirement-planning/602043/how-to-spot-and-squash-nasty-fees-that-hide-in-your

when you are investing for the long term. When the market is trending up, if you are consistently paying in money, month over month, great; your investments can grow, and you are adding to your assets. When the market takes a dip, no problem; your dollars buy more shares at a lower price. At some point, we hope the market will rebound, in which case your shares can grow and possibly be more valuable than they were before. This concept is what we call "dollar-cost averaging." While it can't ensure a profit or guarantee against losses, it's a time-tested strategy for investing in a volatile market.

However, when you are in retirement, this strategy may work against you. You may have heard of "reverse" dollar-cost averaging. Before, when the market lost ground, you were "bargain-shopping"; your dollars purchased more assets at a reduced price. When you are in retirement, you are no longer the purchaser; you are selling. So, in a down market, you have to sell more assets to make the same amount of money as what you made in a favorable market.

I've had lots of people step into my office to talk to me about this, emphasizing, "my advisor says the market always bounces back, and I have to just hold on for the long term."

There's some basis for this thinking; thus far, the market has always rebounded to higher heights than before. But this is no guarantee, and the prospect of potentially higher returns in five years may not be very helpful in retirement if you are relying on the income from those returns to pay this month's electric bill, for example.

For that very reason, I discuss market volatility constantly. During each plan review, we examine how a portfolio is invested and talk about risk exposure.

I also explain what I think will happen in the future, no matter how bright or gloomy the horizon may appear. If conditions don't look good, I let people know to buckle in because volatility is coming or could be here to stay for a while.

We regularly discuss how portfolios typically react during poor markets because it helps allay fears. Clients aren't nearly as anxious during times of volatility when they know their portfolio is reacting as expected and are confident a downturn won't force them to postpone retirement, come out of retirement, or change their lifestyle.

As I noted before, volatility is very much a natural and expected part of market investing. My job is to convey that—clearly.

This is also where having a customized comprehensive plan is invaluable. If your portfolio is down 15 percent, you may not feel good about it. But when you can look at your plan and see that you can still receive all of the immediate income you need for your lifestyle and still have plenty of resources for income later, you are not as concerned about the natural ebbs and flows of the markets.

A lot of confidence comes from seeing that you can continue to live retirement like you planned and that you don't have to come out of retirement because of something you can't control—the markets.

Is There a "Perfect" Product?

To bring us back around to the discussion of protection, growth, and liquidity, the ideal product would be a "ten" in all three categories, right? Completely guaranteed, doubling in size every few years, and accessible whenever you want. Does such a product exist? Absolutely not.

Instead of running in circles looking for that perfect product, the silver bullet, the unicorn of financial strategies, it's more important to circle back to the concept of a balanced, asset-diverse portfolio.

This is why your interests may be best served when you work with a trusted retirement planner who knows what various financial products can do and how to use them in your personal retirement strategy.

CHAPTER 4

Retirement Income

Retirement. For many of us, it's what we've saved for and dreamed of, pinning our hopes to a magical someday. Is that someday full of traveling? Is it filled with grandkids? Gardening? Maybe your fondest dream is simply never having to work again, never having to clock in or be accountable to someone else.

Your ability to do these things all hinges on *income*. Without the money to support these dreams, even a basic level of work-free lifestyle is unsustainable. That's why planning for your income in retirement is so foundational. But where do we begin?

It's easy to feel overwhelmed by this question. Some may feel the urge to amass a large lump sum and then try to put it all in one product—insurance, investments, liquid assets—to provide all the growth, liquidity, and income they need. Instead, I think you need a more balanced approach. After all, retirement planning isn't magic. Like I mention elsewhere, there is no single product that can be all things to all people (or even all things to one person). No approach works unilaterally for everyone. That's why it's important to talk to a retirement planner who can help you lay down the basics and take you step-by-step through the process. Not only will you have the assurance you have addressed the areas you need to, but you will also have an ally who can help you break down the process and help keep you from feeling overwhelmed.

Sources of Income

Thinking of all the pieces of your retirement expenses might be intimidating. But, like cleaning out a junk drawer or revisiting that garage remodel, once you have laid everything out, you can begin to sort things into categories.

Once you have a good overall picture of where your expenses will lie, you can start stacking up the resources to cover them.

Social Security

Social Security is a guaranteed, inflation-protected federal insurance program playing a significant part in most of our retirement plans. From delaying until you've reached full retirement age or beyond to examining spousal benefits, as I discuss elsewhere in this book, there is plenty you can do to try to make the most of this monthly benefit. As with all your retirement income sources, it's important to consider how to make this resource stretch to provide the most bang and buck for your situation.

Pension

Another generally reliable source of retirement income for you might be a pension, if you are one of the lucky people who still has one.

If you don't have a pension, go ahead and skim on to the next section. If you do have a pension, keep on reading.

Because your pension can be such a central piece of your retirement income plan, you will want to put some thought into answering basic questions about it.

How well is your pension funded? Since the heyday of the pension plan, companies and governments have neglected to fund their pension obligations, causing a persistent problem with this otherwise reliable asset.

Consider the factors at play, though. Pensions had been underfunded and gained a boost from strong market performance in 2021. What happens to the solvency of those pension funds if the market declines?

It can be worthwhile to keep tabs on your pension's health and know what your options are for withdrawing your pension. If you have already retired and made those decisions, this may be a foregone conclusion. If not, it pays to know what you can expect and what decisions you can make, such as taking spousal options to cover your husband or wife if he or she outlives you.

Also, some companies are incentivizing lump-sum payouts of pensions to reduce the companies' payment liabilities. If that's the case with your employer, talk to your financial professional to see if it might be prudent to do something like that or if it might be better to stick with lifetime payments or other options.

Your 401(k) and IRA

One "modern way" to save for retirement is in a 401(k) or IRA (or their nonprofit or governmental equivalents). These tax-advantaged accounts are, in my opinion, a poor substitute for pensions, but one of the biggest disservices we do to ourselves is to not take full advantage of them in the first place. According to one article, only 41 percent of Americans invest in a 401(k), though 68 percent of employed Americans have access to a 401(k) benefit option.[19]

Also, if you have changed jobs over the years, do the work of tracking down any benefits from your past employers. You might have an IRA here or a 401(k) there; keep track of those so you can pull them together and look at those assets when you're ready to look at establishing sources of retirement income.

---

[19] Amin Dabit. personalcapital.com. April 1, 2021. "The Average 401k Balance by Age." https://www.personalcapital.com/blog/retirement-planning/average-401k-balance-age/

Do You Have...

- Life insurance?
- Annuities?
- Long-term care insurance?
- Any passive income sources?
- Stock and bond portfolios?
- Liquid assets? (What's in your bank account?)
- Alternative investments?
- Rental properties?

If you are going through the work of sitting with a retirement planner, it's important to look at your full retirement income picture and pull together *all* your assets, no matter how big or small. From the free insurance policy offered at your bank to the sizable investment in your brother-in-law's modestly successful furniture store, you want to have a good idea of where your money is.

A single woman—we can call her Sue—once came to me when she was sixty-three. Sue wanted to retire at age sixty-five and said she thought she only needed about $3,500 per month to live her desired lifestyle in retirement. Sue wanted to know if her retirement resources would provide for that long term.

We started working together and building Sue's retirement plan. As we organized and consolidated her investments and determined the best choice for her Social Security, we built a plan that could generate $3,500 of monthly guaranteed lifetime income as soon as she retired. Just two short years into retirement, her retirement plan would be able to generate $5,000 a month of guaranteed income. Then, five years into retirement, her plan would generate $7,500 of monthly guaranteed income that she could never outlive.

Sue had no idea she could generate that kind of income from her retirement resources, let alone have it guaranteed for life. We also were able to build in inflation adjustments, so the $7,500 per month wasn't the only income she would receive fifteen or twenty years into retirement. In other words, we developed a plan that would always provide Sue with the equivalent of $7,500 a month in today's dollars to support her lifestyle, even if life's price tag increased.

As you can imagine, Sue was relieved she could retire in two years and was very excited that she would enjoy a better lifestyle in retirement than she ever imagined.

Retirement Income Needs

How much income will you need in retirement? How do you determine that? A lot of people work toward a random number, thinking, "If I can just have a million dollars, I'll be comfortable in retirement!" Don't get me wrong; it is possible to save up a lot of money and then retire in the hopes you can keep your monthly expenses lower than some set estimation. But I think this carries a general risk of running out of money. Instead, I work with my clients to find out what their current and projected income needs are and then work from there to see how we might cover any gaps between what they have and what they want.

Goals and Dreams

I like to start with your pie in the sky. Do you find yourself planning for your vacations more thoroughly than you do your retirement? It's not uncommon for Americans to spend more time planning our vacations than we spend planning our retirements. Maybe it's because planning a vacation is less stressful: Having a week at the beach go awry is, well, a walk on the beach compared to running out of money in retirement. Whatever the case, perhaps it would be better if you thought of your retirement as a vacation in and of itself—no clocking in, no boss, no overtime. If you felt unlimited by financial strain, what would you do?

Would an endless vacation for you mean Paris and Rome? Would it mean mentoring at children's clubs or serving at the local soup kitchen? Or maybe it would mean deepening your ties to those immediately around you—neighbors, friends, and family. Maybe it would mean more time to take part in the hobbies and activities you love. Have you been considering a second (or even third) act as a small-business owner, turning a hobby or passion into a revenue source?

This is your time to daydream and answer the question: If you could do anything, what would you do?

After that, it's a matter of putting a dollar amount on it. What are the costs of round-the-world travel? One couple I know said their highest priority in retirement was being able to take each of their grandchildren on a cross-country vacation every year. That's a pretty specific goal—one that is reasonably easy to nail down a budget for.

There are plenty of other stories, to be sure. Consider the couple I met about ten years ago.

They were in their late fifties and feeling like work was beating them up daily. They'd had some people close to them pass away and were feeling like they needed to start experiencing retirement while they still could. However, they were insecure about the money they had saved. They weren't sure it was enough, partly because they had seen information indicating they couldn't retire well even with a million dollars. They had far less than that.

One of their retirement dreams was to buy a motor home and travel the country. The motor home they were looking at was just under $100,000.

We built their plan with all of this in mind. Their plan was designed to have their pension be the foundational source of funding for their day-to-day lifestyle, with a little help from their investments until they were able to turn on Social Security. We also used their investments to fund the financing of the motor home.

They retired and started traveling the country. They told us about all the new friends they were making along the way and sent us pictures of the sites they visited. They discovered they really enjoyed having the freedom just to pick up and go wherever their hearts desired.

Today, ten years later, they are still traveling and still living their best life with little concern about their retirement funding, because they have a written retirement plan that shows them that it all works, how it all works, and why it all works.

Current Budget

Compiling a current expense report is one of the trickiest pieces of retirement preparation. Many people assume the expenses of their lives in retirement will be different—lower. After all, there will be no drive to work, no need for a formal wardrobe, and, perhaps most impactful of all, no more saving for retirement!

Yet, we often underestimate our daily spending habits. That's why I typically ask my clients to bring in their bank statements for the past year—they reflect your *actual* spending, not just what you think you're spending.

We look at our clients' checking accounts, credit cards, and other ways they've spent money for the past twelve months. We then calculate how much was spent, subtracting bigger, one-time expenses such as major home repairs or car purchases. The final number represents the cost of their current lifestyle.

We then talk them through the spending experience a lot of retirees go through. We start this process by asking them what days of the week they spend most of their lifestyle money. Many people choose the weekends, because they aren't working on those days.

"Well," we tell them, "In retirement, every day of the week is a weekend." During retirement, you will have more free time than you've had in decades. Therefore, many retirees often spend more during the go-go years of their retirement than during the last few years of their work careers.

So, whatever their lifestyle cost is at the time of retirement, we might want to add 10 to 15 percent to it for a few years, just to be safe. After all, not too many people want to retire and then be forced to cut back on the activities they love to do.

I can't count the number of times I have sat with a couple, asked them about their spending, and heard them throw out a number that seemed incredibly low. When I ask them where the number came from, they usually say they estimated based on their total bills. Yet, our spending is so much more than our mortgage, utilities, cable, phone, car, grocery, or credit card bills.

"What about clothes?" I ask, "Or dining out? What about gifts and coffees and last-minute birthday cards?" That's when the lights come on.

This is why I suggest collecting a year's worth of information. There is usually no such thing as a one-time purchase. Did you buy new furniture? Even if that is a rarity, do you think that will be the last time you *ever* buy furniture?

Many people within ten years of retiring (their Redzone to Retirement), make more money than they ever have made and have less debt than ever. Their discretionary income is at an all-time high.

They may have had to live on a budget for many years, but for the past five to ten years, they haven't had to stress about a strict budget. As a result, they often don't know exactly how much income it takes to live their current lifestyle.

Recently, I asked a couple who started working with us about these numbers, and their estimate was about $6,500 a month. I asked them to go back over their past twelve months of expenses just to make sure. After they removed a few one-off expenses that they won't have in most years, their normal month-to-month living costs were actually $9,000.

This was an important revelation because if we had used $6,500 instead of $9,000 while building their strategy, much of their plan would have been off track. Their tax and income plans would have looked much different.

These are the types of surprises we need to eliminate before you retire. The sooner you know what it really is going to cost you to retire your way, the more likely it will be for us to put together a plan to accomplish your lifestyle goals.

Another hefty expense is spending on the kids. Many of the couples I work with are quick to help their adult children, whether it's something like letting them live in the basement, paying for college, babysitting, paying an occasional bill, or contributing to a grandchild's college fund. Research concluded that 22 percent of adults receive some kind of financial support from parents. That segment jumps to almost 30 percent when factoring the generation we call millennials.[20]

My clients sometimes protest that what they do for their grown children can stop in retirement. They don't *need* to help. But I get it. Parents like to feel needed. And, while you never want to neglect saving for retirement in favor of taking on financial risks (like your child's student debt), the parents who help their adult children do so in part because it helps them feel fulfilled.

When it comes down to expenses, including (and especially) spending on your family, don't make your initial calculations based on what you *could* whittle your budget down to if you *had* to. Instead, start from where you are. Who wants to live off a bare-bones bank account in retirement?

Other Expenses

Once you have nailed down your current budget and your dreams or goals for retirement, there are a few other outstanding pieces to think about—some expenses many people don't take the time to consider before making and executing a plan. But I'm assuming you want to get it right, so let's take a look.

---

[20] Kamaron McNair. magnifymoney.com. October 26, 2021. "Nearly 30% of Millenials Still Receive Financial Support From Their Parents" https://www.magnifymoney.com/blog/news/parental-financial-support-survey/

Housing

Do you know where you want to live in retirement? This makes up a substantial piece of your income puzzle—since the typical American household owns a home, and it's generally their largest asset.

Some people prefer to live right where they are for as long as they can. Others have been waiting for retirement to pull the trigger on an ambitious move, like purchasing a new house, or even downsizing. Whatever your plans and whatever your reasons, there are quite a few things to consider.

Mortgage

Do you still have a mortgage? What may have been a nice tax boon in your working years could turn into a financial burden in your retirement. After all, when you are on a limited income, a mortgage is just one more bill sapping your financial strength. It is something to put some thought into, whether you plan to age in place or are considering moving to your dream home, buying a house out of state, or living in a retirement community.

Upkeep and Taxes

A house without a mortgage still requires annual taxes. While it's tempting to think of this as a once-a-year expense, when you have limited earning potential, your annual tax bill might be something into which you should put a little more forethought.

The costs of homeownership aren't just monetary. When you find yourself dealing with more house than you need, it can drain your time and energy. From keeping clutter at bay to keeping the lawn mower running, upkeep can be extensive and expensive. For some, that's a challenge they heartily accept and can comfortably take on. For others, the idea of yard work or cleaning an area larger than they need feels foolish.

For instance, Peggy discovered after her knee replacement that most of her house was inaccessible to her when she was laid up.

"It felt ridiculous to pay someone else to dust and vacuum a house I was only living in 40 percent of!"

Practicality and Adaptability

Phil and Joan are looking to retire within the next two decades. They just sold their old three-bedroom ranch-style house. Their twins are in high school, and the couple has wanted to "upgrade" for years. Now they live in a gorgeous 1940s three-story house with all the kitchen space they ever wanted, five sprawling bedrooms, and a library and media room for themselves and their children. Within months of moving in, the couple realized a house perfect for their active teens would no longer be perfect for them in five to fifteen years.

"We are paying the mortgage for this house, but we've started saving for the next one," said Joan, "because who wants to climb two flights of stairs to their bedroom when they're seventy-eight?"

Others I know have encountered a similar situation in their personal lives. After a health crisis, one couple found the luxurious tub for two they toiled to install had become a specter of a bad slip and a potential safety risk. It's important to think through what your physical reality could be. I always emphasize to my clients that they should plan for whatever their long-term future might hold.

Contracts and Regulations

If you are looking into a cross-country move, be aware of new tax tables or local ordinances in the area where you are looking to move. After all, you don't want to experience sticker-shock when you are looking at downsizing or reducing your bills in retirement.

Along the same lines, if you are moving into a retirement community, be sure to look at the fine print. What happens if you must move into a different situation for long-term care? Will you be penalized? Will you be responsible for replacing your slot in the community? What are all the fees, and what do they cover?

Inflation

As I write this in 2023, America has experienced a wave of inflation following a lengthy period of low inflation. Inflation zoomed to 9.1 percent in June 2022, its highest mark since November 1981.[21]

Core inflation is yet another measurement that excludes goods with prices that tend to be more volatile, such as food and energy costs. Core inflation for a 12-month period ending in December 2022 was 5.7 percent. It so happened energy prices rose7.3 percent over that timeframe.[22]

However, inflation isn't a one-time bump; it has a cumulative effect. Again, that can impact the price of groceries greater than other goods. Even with relatively low inflation over the past few decades, an item you bought in 1997 for two dollars will cost about $3.70 today.[23] Want to go to a show? A $20 ticket in 1997 would cost $41.24 in 2022.[24]

What if, in retirement, we hit a stretch like the late seventies and early eighties, when annual inflation rates of 10 percent became the norm? It may be wise to consider some extra padding in your retirement income plan to account for any potential increase in inflation in the future.

---

[21] tradingeconomics.com. 2022 Data/2023 Forecast/1914-2021 Historical. "United States Inflation Rate" https://tradingeconomics.com/united-states/inflation-cpi

[22] U.S. Inflation Calculator. "United States Core Inflation Rates (1957-2022)" https://www.usinflationcalculator.com/inflation/united-states-core-inflation-rates/

[23] In2013dollars.com. "$2 in 1997 is worth $3.70 today" https://www.in2013dollars.com/us/inflation/1997?amount=2

[24] In2013dollars.com "Admission to movies, theaters, and concerts priced at $20 in 1997>$40.34 in 2022" https://www.in2013dollars.com/Admission-to-movies,-theaters,-and-concerts/price-inflation

Aging

Also, in the expense category, think about longevity. We all hope to age gracefully. However, it's important to face the prospect of aging with a sense of realism.

The elephant in the room for many families is long-term care. No one wants to admit they will likely need it, but estimates indicate almost 70 percent of us will.[25] Aging is a significant piece of retirement income planning because you'll want to figure out how to set aside money for your care, either at home or away from it. The more comfortable you get with discussing your wishes and plans with your loved ones, the easier planning for the financial side of it can be.

I denote health care and potential long-term care costs in more detail elsewhere in this book, but suffice it to say nursing home care tends to be very expensive and typically isn't something you get to choose when you will need.

It isn't just the costs of long-term care that pose a concern in living longer. It's also about covering the possible costs of everything else associated with living longer. For instance, if Henry retires from his job as a biochemical engineer at age sixty-five, perhaps he planned to have a very decent income for twenty years, until age eighty-five. But what if he lives until he's ninety-five? That's a whole third—ten years—more of personal income he will need.

Putting It All Together

Whew! So, you have pulled together what you have, and you have a pretty good idea of where you want to be. Now your retirement planner and you can go about the work of arranging what assets you *have* to cover what you *need*—and how you might try to cover any gaps.

---

25 Moll Law Group. 2022. "The Cost of Long-Term Care." https://www.molllawgroup.com/the-cost-of-long-term-care.html

Like the proverbial man in the Bible who built his house on a rock, I like to help my clients figure out how to cover their day-to-day living expenses—their needs—with insurance and other guaranteed income sources like pensions and Social Security.

In doing that, we build a customized written retirement plan for every client we help. We call it **Your Merkle Plan**, and it includes six distinct components:

- Lifestyle Plan
- Income Plan
- Tax Plan
- Health Care Plan
- Legacy Plan
- Investment Plan

Your Merkle Plan clearly demonstrates when you can retire, how much you can spend monthly and yearly, and how likely you are to run out of money or have plenty of money to enjoy *all* parts of your retirement.

The power of a written plan simply can't be overstated. We don't just sit across the table and tell you that you can retire. Instead, we tell you and show you at the same time. When you can see how much you can spend, the sources of your income, and how long your money will last, you quickly become empowered to make retirement decisions with a lot more confidence.

Again, you should keep in mind there isn't one single financial vehicle, asset, or source to fill all your needs, and that's okay. One of the challenges of planning for your income in retirement concerns figuring out what products and strategies to use. You can release some of that stress when you accept the fact you will probably need a diverse portfolio—potentially with bonds, stocks, insurance, and other income sources—not just one massive money pile.

One way to help shore up your income gaps is by working with your retirement planner and a qualified tax advisor to mitigate your tax exposure. If you have a 401(k) or IRA, a tax advisor in your corner can help you figure out how and when to take distributions from your account in a way that doesn't push you into a higher tax bracket. Or you might learn how to use tax-advantaged bonds more effectively. Effective tax planning isn't necessarily about "adding" to your income. Especially regarding retirement, it's less about what you make than it is about what you keep. Paying a lower tax bill keeps more money in your pocket, which is where you want it when it comes to retirement income.

Now you can look at ways to cover your remaining retirement goals. Are there products like long-term care insurance specific to a certain kind of expense you anticipate? Is there a particular asset you want to use for your "play" money—money for trips and gifts for the grandkids? Is there any way you can portion off money for those charitable legacy plans?

Once you have analyzed your income wants, needs, and the assets to realistically cover them, you may have a gap. The masterstroke of a competent financial professional will be to help you figure out how you will cover that gap. Will you need to cut out a round of golf a week? Maybe skip the new car? Or will you need to take more substantial action?

One way to cover an income gap is to consider working longer or even part-time before retirement and even after that magical calendar date. This may not be the best "plan" for you; disabilities, work demands, and physical or emotional limitations can hinder the best-laid plans to continue working. However, if it is physically possible for you, this is one considerable way to help your assets last, for more than one reason.

In fact, 46 percent of the Americans responding to a survey report they plan to work part-time after retiring, while 18 percent indicated they planned to work past the age of seventy.[26]

---

[26] Palash Ghosh. Forbes.com. May 6, 2021. "A Third Of Seniors Seek To Work Well Past Retirement Age, Or Won't Retire At All, Poll Finds"

When you're retired, you no longer have an employer paying you a steady check. It is up to you to make sure you have saved and planned for the income you need.

And it's up to people like me to help. That's why one of the greatest joys I get is seeing someone pick up their **Your Merkle Plan** for the first time and realize they can retire and live the lifestyle that they want.

I'll never forget the gentleman we met a while back. Stressed to the max and in his early sixties, his blood pressure was understandably high. His doctor told him he had to change his lifestyle, including eating habits, and find a way to relieve the stress. Otherwise, he could encounter some serious heart issues.

He told us the pressures of his job were too much and that he had to find a way out. He also said he loved the outdoors and wanted to walk away from work and be outdoors with nature as much as possible. However, he didn't think he could do this because he hadn't saved for retirement like he thought he should have.

We got right to work. We built his retirement plan and found a way for him to retire and start enjoying the outdoors within twelve months. He followed the plan's steps diligently, and sure enough, retired a year later.

I saw him for a plan review six months after he retired, and he looked great. He felt great, too, and told me his last doctor's appointment was the best one he'd had in years. His blood pressure was way down, and he said he was as relaxed as he could ever remember. Best of all, he was living his retirement dream!

---

https://www.forbes.com/sites/palashghosh/2021/05/06/a-third-of-seniors-seek-to-work-well-past-retirement-age-or-wont-retire-at-all-poll-finds/?sh=1d2ece836b95

CHAPTER 5

Social Security

S ocial Security is often the foundation of retirement income. Backed by the strength of the U.S. Treasury, it provides perhaps the most dependable paycheck you will have in retirement.

From the time you collect your first paycheck from the job that made you a bonafide taxpayer, you are paying into the grand old Social Security system. For me, that was working in the Hy-Vee deli as a senior in high school for $5.15 per hour (if I remember correctly). I'd bus tables, prepare food, do dishes—basically anything that was required to keep the deli running smoothly. On a really good day, someone might even leave a dime or quarter tip on the table I was cleaning. Even though it wasn't much, I remember being grateful and thinking, "Every little bit helps."

What grew and developed out of the pressures of the Great Depression has become one of the most popular government programs in the country, and, if you pay in for the equivalent of ten years or more, you, too, can benefit from the Social Security program.

Now, before we get into the nitty-gritty of Social Security, I'd like to address a current concern: Will Social Security still be there for you when you reach retirement age?

The Future of Social Security

This question is ever-present as headlines trumpet an underfunded Social Security program, alongside the sea of baby boomers retiring in droves and the comparatively smaller pool of younger people who are funding the system.

The Social Security Administration itself acknowledges this concern as each Social Security statement now contains a link to its website (ssa.gov) and a page entitled, "Will Social Security Be There For Me?"

Just a reminder, as if you needed one, that nothing in life is guaranteed. Additionally, depending on who you're listening to, Social Security funds may run low before 2034, thanks to the financial instability and government spending that accompanied the 2020 COVID-19 pandemic.

Before you get too discouraged, though, here are a few thoughts to keep you going:

- Even if the program is only paying 78 cents on the dollar for scheduled benefits, 78 percent is notably not zero.
- The Social Security Administration has made changes in the distant and near past to protect the fund's solvency, including increasing retirement ages and striking certain filing strategies.
- There are many changes Congress could make, and lawmakers routinely discuss how to fix the system, such as further increasing full retirement age and eligibility.
- One thing no one is seriously discussing? Reneging on current obligations to retirees or the soon-to-retire.

Take heart. The real answer to the question, "Will Social Security be there for me?" is still yes.

This question is important to consider when you look at how much we, as a nation, rely on this program. Did you know Social

Security benefits replace about 40 percent of a person's original income when they retire?[27]

If you ask me, that's a pretty significant piece of your retirement income puzzle.

Another caveat? You may not realize this, but no one can legally "advise" you about your Social Security benefits.

"But, Loren," you may be thinking, "isn't that part of what you do? And what about that nice gentleman at the Social Security Administration office I spoke with on the phone?"

Don't get me wrong. Social Security Administration employees know their stuff. They are trained to understand policies and programs, and they are usually pretty quick to tell you what you can and cannot do. But the government specifically stipulates, because Social Security is a benefit you alone have paid into and earned, your Social Security decisions, too, are yours alone.

When it comes to financial professionals, we can't push you in any direction, but—there's a big but here—working with a well-informed retirement planner is still incredibly handy for your Social Security decisions. Why? Because in Your Merkle Plan, we can show you how making different Social Security decisions can impact your overall plan, including your tax, investment, income, and even your legacy plans.

With Social Security being such a meaningful source of income, you want to make sure you get it right. Seeing how your decisions can influence your overall plan can give you the confidence you need to make this decision and feel really good about it. Whatever your reasons, questions, or feelings regarding Social Security, the decision is yours alone. However, working with a retirement planner can help you put your options in perspective by showing you—both with industry knowledge and with proprietary software or planning

---

[27] ssa.gov. "Alternate Measure of Replacement Rates for Social Security Benefits and Retirement Income"
https://www.ssa.gov/policy/docs/ssb/v68n2/v68n2p1.html.

processes—where your benefits fit into your overall strategy for retirement income.

One reason the federal government doesn't allow for "advice" related to Social Security, I suspect, is so no one can profit from giving you advice related to your Social Security benefit—or from providing any clarifications. Again, this is a sign of a good retirement planner. Those who are passionate about their work will be knowledgeable about what benefit strategies might be to your advantage and will happily share those possible options with you.

Full Retirement Age

When it comes to Social Security, it seems like many people only think so far as "yes." They don't take the time to understand the various options available. Instead, because it is common knowledge you can begin your benefits at age sixty-two, that's what many people do. While more people are opting to delay taking benefits, age sixty-two is still firmly the most popular age to start.[28]

However, by starting benefits early, they may be leaving a lot of money on the table. You see, the Social Security Administration bases your monthly benefit on two factors: your earnings history and your full retirement age (FRA).

From your earnings history, they pull the thirty-five years you made the most money and use a mathematical indexing formula to figure out a monthly average from those years. If you paid into the system for less than thirty-five years, then every year you didn't pay in will be counted as a zero.

Once it calculates what your monthly earnings would be at FRA, the government calculates what to put on your check based on how close you are to FRA. FRA was originally set at

---

[28] Chris Kissell. moneytalknews.com. January 20, 2021. "This Is When the Most People Start Taking Social Security." https://www.moneytalksnews.com/the-most-popular-age-for-claiming-social-security/

sixty-five, but as the population aged and lifespans lengthened, the government shifted FRA later and later, based on an individual's year of birth. Check out the following chart to see when you will reach FRA.[29]

Age to Receive Full Social Security Benefits*	
(Called "full retirement age" [FRA] or "normal retirement age.")	
Year of Birth*	FRA
1937 or earlier	65
1938	65 and 2 months
1939	65 and 4 months
1940	65 and 6 months
1941	65 and 8 months
1942	65 and 10 months
1943-1954	66
1955	66 and 2 months
1956	66 and 4 months
1957	66 and 6 months
1958	66 and 8 months
1959	66 and 10 months
1960 and later	67

*If you were born on Jan. 1 of any year, you should refer to the previous year. (If you were born on the 1st of the month, we figure your benefit [and your full retirement age] as if your birthday was in the previous month.)

When you reach FRA, you are eligible to receive 100 percent of whatever the Social Security Administration says is your full monthly benefit.

Starting at age sixty-two, for every year before FRA you claim benefits, your monthly check is reduced by 5 percent or more. Conversely, for every year you delay taking benefits past FRA, your monthly benefit increases by 8 percent (until age seventy—after that, there is no monetary advantage to delaying Social Security benefits). While your circumstances and needs may vary, a lot of financial professionals still urge people to at least consider delaying until they reach age seventy.

Why wait?[30]

Taking benefits early could affect your monthly check by _____.								
62	63	64	65	FRA 66	67	68	69	70
-25 %	-20 %	-13.3 %	-6.7 %	0	+8 %	+16 %	+24 %	+32 %

My Social Security

If you are over age thirty, you have probably received a notice from the Social Security Administration telling you to activate something called "My Social Security." This is a handy way to learn more about your particular benefit options, to keep track of what your earnings record looks like, and to calculate the benefits you have accrued over the years.

Essentially, My Social Security is an online account you can activate to see what your personal Social Security picture looks like, which you can do at www.ssa.gov/myaccount. This can be extremely helpful when it comes to planning for income in retirement and figuring up the difference between your anticipated income versus anticipated expenses.

---

[30] Social Security Administration. April 2021. "Can You Take Your Benefits Before Full Retirement Age?"
https://www.ssa.gov/planners/retire/applying2.html

COLA

Social Security is a largely guaranteed piece of the retirement puzzle: If you get a statement that reads you should expect $1,000 a month, you can be sure you will receive $1,000 a month. But there is one variable detail, and that is something called the cost-of-living adjustment, or COLA.

The COLA is an increase in your monthly check meant to address inflation in everyday life. After all, your expenses will likely continue to experience inflation in retirement, but you will no longer have the opportunity for raises, bonuses, or promotions you had when you were working. Instead, Social Security receives an annual cost-of-living increase tied to the Department of Labor's Consumer Price Index for Urban Wage Earners and Clerical Workers, or CPI-W. If the CPI-W measurement shows inflation rose a certain amount for regular goods and services, then Social Security recipients will see that reflected in their COLA.

COLA adjustments have climbed as high as 14.3 percent (1980) and in 2023 reached 8.7 percent, the largest increase in more than forty years. But in a no- or low-inflation environment, such as in 2010, 2011, and 2016, Social Security recipients will not receive an adjustment.[31] Some view the COLA as a perk, bump, or bonus, but, in reality, it works more like this: Your mom sends you to the store with $2.50 for a gallon of milk. Milk costs exactly $2.50. The next week, you go back with that same amount, but it is now $2.52 for a gallon, so you go back to Mom, and she gives you 2 cents. You aren't bringing home more milk—it just costs more money.

So the COLA is less about "making more money" and more about keeping seniors' purchasing power from eroding when inflation is a big factor, such as in 1975, when it was 8 percent![32] Still, don't let that detract from your enthusiasm about COLAs;

---

[31] ssa.gov. "Cost-Of-Living Adjustments" ssa.gov/oact/cola/colaseries.html
[32] Social Security Administration. "Cost-Of-Living Adjustment (COLA) Information for 2022." https://www.ssa.gov/cola/

after all, what if Mom's solution was: "Here's the same $2.50; try to find pennies from somewhere else to get that milk!"?

Spousal Benefits

We've talked about FRA, but another big Social Security decision involves spousal benefits.

If you or your spouse has a long stretch of zeros in your earnings history—perhaps if one of you stayed home for years, caring for children or sick relatives—you may want to consider filing for spousal benefits instead of filing on your own earnings history. A spousal benefit can be up to 50 percent of the primary wage earner's benefit at full retirement age.

To begin drawing a spousal benefit, you must be at least sixty-two years old, and the primary wage earner must have already filed for his or her benefit. While there are penalties for taking spousal benefits early, you cannot earn credits for delaying past full retirement age.[33]

Like I wrote, the spousal benefit can be a big deal for those who don't have a very long pay history, but it's important to weigh your own earned benefits against the option of withdrawing based on a fraction of your spouse's benefits.

To look at how this could play out, let's use a hypothetical couple: Mary, who is sixty, and Peter, who is sixty-two.

Let's say Peter's benefit at FRA, in his case sixty-seven, would be $1,600. If Peter begins his benefits right now, four years before FRA, his monthly check will be $1,200. If Mary begins taking spousal benefits in two years at the earliest date possible, her monthly benefits will be reduced by 67.5 percent, to $520 per month (remember, at FRA, the most she can qualify for is half of Peter's FRA benefit).

What if Peter and Mary both wait until FRA? At sixty-seven, Peter begins taking his full benefit of $1,600 a month. Two years later, when she reaches age sixty-seven, Mary will qualify

---

33 Social Security Administration. "Retirement Planner: Benefits For You As A Spouse." https://www.ssa.gov/planners/retire/applying6.html

for $800 a month. By waiting until FRA, the couple's monthly benefit goes from $1,720 to $2,400.

What if Peter delays until age seventy to get his maximum possible benefit? For each year past FRA he delays, his monthly benefits increase by 8 percent. This means, at seventy, he could file for a monthly benefit of $2,015. However, delayed retirement credits do not affect spousal benefits, so as soon as Peter files at seventy, Mary would also file (at age sixty-eight) for her maximum benefit of $800, so their highest possible combined monthly check is $2,815.[34]

When it comes to your Social Security benefits, you obviously will want to consider whether a monthly check based on a fraction of your spouse's earnings will be comparable to or larger than your own earnings history.

Divorced Spouses

There are a few considerations for those of us who have gone through a divorce. If you 1) were married for ten years or more *and* 2) have since been divorced for at least two years *and* 3) are unmarried *and* 4) your ex-spouse qualifies to begin Social Security, you qualify for a spousal benefit based on your ex-husband or ex-wife's earnings history at FRA. A divorced spousal benefit is different from the married spousal benefit in one way: You don't have to wait for your ex-spouse to file before you can file yourself.[35]

For instance, Charles and Lora were married for fifteen years before their divorce, when he was thirty-six and she was forty. Lora has been remarried for twenty years, and, although Charles briefly remarried, his second marriage ended after a few years. Charles' benefits are largely calculated based on his

---

34 Office of the Chief Actuary. Social Security Administration. "Social Security Benefits: Benefits for Spouses."
https://www.ssa.gov/OACT/quickcalc/spouse.html#calculator
35 Social Security Administration. "Retirement Planner: If You Are Divorced." https://www.ssa.gov/planners/retire/divspouse.html

many years of volunteering in schools, meaning his personal monthly benefit is close to zero.

Although Lora has deferred her retirement, opting to delay benefits until she is seventy, Charles can begin taking benefits calculated from Lora's work history at FRA as early as sixty-two. However, he will also have the option of waiting until FRA to collect the maximum, or 50 percent of Lora's earned monthly benefit at her FRA.

Widowed Spouses

If your marriage ended with the death of your spouse, you might claim a benefit for your spouse's earned income as his or her widow/widower, called a survivor's benefit. Unlike a spousal benefit or divorced benefits, if your husband or wife dies, you can claim his or her full benefit. Also, unlike spousal benefits, if you need to, you can begin taking income when you turn sixty. However, as with other benefit options, your monthly check will be permanently reduced for withdrawing benefits before FRA.

If your spouse began taking benefits before he or she died, you can't delay withdrawing your survivor's benefits to get delayed credits. The Social Security Administration maintains you can only get as much from a survivor's benefit as your deceased spouse might have received, had he or she lived.[36]

Taxes, Taxes, Taxes

With Social Security, as with everything, it is important to consider taxes. It may be surprising, but your Social Security benefits are not tax-free. Despite having been taxed to accrue those benefits in the first place, you may have to pay the IRS income taxes on up to 85 percent of your Social Security.

---

[36] Social Security Administration. "Social Security Benefit Amounts For The Surviving Spouse By Year Of Birth." https://www.ssa.gov/planners/survivors/survivorchartred.html

The Social Security Administration figures these taxes using what they call "the provisional income formula." Your provisional income formula differs from the adjusted gross income you use for your regular income taxes. Instead, to find out how much of your Social Security benefit is taxable, the Social Security Administration calculates it this way:

Provisional Income = Adjusted Gross Income + Nontaxable Interest + ½ of Social Security

See that piece about nontaxable interest? That generally means interest from government bonds and notes. It surprises many people that, although you may not pay taxes on those assets, their income will count against you when it comes to Social Security taxation.

Once you have figured out your provisional income (also called "combined income"), you can use the following chart to figure out your Social Security taxes.[37]

---

[37] Social Security Administration. "Benefits Planner: Income Taxes and Your Social Security Benefits." https://www.ssa.gov/planners/taxes.html

Taxes on Social Security		
Provisional Income = Adjusted Gross Income + Nontaxable Interest + ½ of Social Security		
If you are ____ and your provisional income is____, then...		Uncle Sam will tax ___ of your Social Security
Single	Married, filing jointly	
Less than $25,000	Less than $32,000	0%
$25,000 to $34,000	$32,000 to $44,000	Up to 50%
More than $34,000	More than $44,000	Up to 85%

This is one more reason it may benefit you to work with financial and tax professionals. They can look at your entire financial picture to make your overall retirement plan as tax-efficient as possible—including your Social Security benefit.

The key is to decrease your taxable income. One strategy you can use is a Roth IRA conversion, which is what we did for a high-earning client we'll call Mr. Jones.

Mr. Jones filed his taxes as a single, meaning a portion of his Social Security was subject to federal income taxes because he made a six-figure work income, well over the $25,000 provisional income threshold. It didn't make sense for us to do a Roth conversion while Mr. Jones was in a high tax bracket, but when he retired, we turned on Social Security because it is tax-favored.

Because only up to 85 percent of Mr. Jones' Social Security benefits were taxable, we produced some additional retirement income from his portfolio and then used the rest of the 22 percent tax bracket to do Roth conversions. We repeated this process for eight years and converted enough that, by the time he began taking required minimum distributions, his standard deduction covered his RMDs plus some of his Social Security income. We then took the remaining amount of retirement income that Mr. Jones needed from his Roth IRA, which was tax-free.

With this strategy, he paid income tax on his Social Security for eight years, but his Social Security income should be tax-free for the rest of his retirement.

Working and Social Security: The Earnings Test

If you haven't reached FRA, but you started your Social Security benefits and are still working, things get a little hairy.

Because you have started Social Security payments, the Social Security Administration will pay out your benefits (at that reduced rate, of course, because you haven't reached your FRA). Yet, because you are working, the organization must also withhold from your check to add to your benefits, which you are already collecting. See how this complicates matters?

To address the situation, the government has what is called the earnings test. For 2023, you can earn up to $21,240 without it affecting your Social Security check if you're younger than full retirement age. But, for every $2 you earn past that amount, the Social Security Administration will withhold $1. The earnings test loosens in the year of your FRA; if you are reaching FRA in 2023, you can earn up to $56,520 before you run into the earnings test, and the government only withholds $1 for every $3 past that amount.

The month you reach FRA, you are no longer subject to any earnings withholding. For instance, if you are still working and will turn sixty-six on December 28, 2023, you would only have to worry about the earnings test until December, and then you can ignore it entirely. Keep in mind, the money the government withholds from your Social Security benefits while you are working before FRA will be tacked back onto your benefits check after FRA.[38]

If a married couple adds up the monthly benefits they will receive from Social Security over a projected twenty-five-year retirement, they very well could receive $1 million or more. For a single individual, this amount could be over $500,000. It can be a huge benefit for a retiree, so we must take it seriously and investigate all Social Security options.

That means we can't look at Social Security in a vacuum. The decisions retirees make with their Social Security could impact decisions they make with their tax, investment, and income plans.

This is why we don't make any Social Security decisions until we build a full plan. After that, we start experimenting by putting Social Security Decision A into the plan to see what the short- and long-term effects of that decision are on all of the components of the plan. Next, we try Social Security Decision B with the plan, and so on. We keep investigating until all viable Social Security options have been properly vetted. Once our clients see the short- and long-term outcomes of these decisions, their Social Security choice becomes surprisingly simple.

---

[38] Social Security Administration. "Receiving Benefits White Working" https://www.ssa.gov/benefits/retirement/planner/whileworking.html.

CHAPTER 6

401(k)s & IRAs

H ave you heard? Today's retirement is not your parents' retirement. You see, back in the day, it was pretty common to work for one company for the vast majority of your career and then retire with a gold watch and a pension.

The gold watch was a symbol of the quality time you had put in at that company, but the pension was more than a symbol. Instead, it was a guarantee—as solid as your employer—that they would repay your hard work with a certain amount of income in your old age. Did you see the caveat there? Your pension's guarantee was *as solid as your employer.* The problem was, what if your employer went under?

Companies that failed couldn't pay their retired employees' pensions, leading to financial challenges for many. Beginning in 1974 with Congress' passage of the Employee Retirement Income Security Act, federal legislation and regulations aimed at protecting retirees were everywhere. One piece of legislation included a relatively obscure section of the Internal Revenue Code, added in 1978. Section 401(k), to be specific.

IRC section 401, subsection k, created tax advantages for employer-sponsored financial products, even if the main contributor was the employee him or herself. Over the years, more employers took note, beginning an age of transition away from pensions and toward 401(k) plans. A 401(k) is a retirement account with certain tax benefits and restrictions on the investments or other financial products inside of it.

Essentially, 401(k)s and their individual retirement account (IRA) counterparts are "wrappers" that provide tax benefits around assets; typically, the assets that compose IRAs and 401(k)s are mutual funds, stock and bond mixes, and money market accounts. However, IRA and 401(k) contents are becoming more diverse these days, with some companies offering different kinds of annuity options within their plans.

Where pensions are defined-*benefit* plans, 401(k)s and IRAs are defined-*contribution* plans. The one-word change outlines the basic difference. Pensions spell out what you can expect to receive from the plan but not necessarily how much money it will take to fund those benefits. With 401(k)s, an employer sets a standard for how much they will contribute (if any), and you can be certain of what you are contributing. Still, there is no outline for what you can expect to receive in return for those contributions.

Modern employment looks very different. A 2022 survey by the Bureau of Labor Statistics determined U.S. workers stayed with their employers a median of 4.1 years. Workers age fifty-five to sixty-four had a little more staying power and were most likely to stay with their employer for about ten years.[39] Participation in 401(k) plans has steadily risen this century, totaling $7.3 trillion in assets in 2021 compared to $3.1 trillion in 2011. The survey revealed about 60 million active participants engaged in 401(k) plans.[40]

Those statistics make it clear that 401(k) plans have replaced pensions at many companies and, for that matter, a gold watch.

Those stats also make it clear that planning for retirement today requires much more foresight and discipline during your working years. Those who won't have the benefit of a pension

---

[39] Bureau of Labor Statistics. September 22, 2022. "Employee Tenure Summary." https://www.bls.gov/news.release/tenure.nr0.htm

[40] Investment Company Institute. October 11, 2021. "Frequently Asked Questions About 401(k) Plan Research" https://www.ici.org/faqs/faq/401k/faqs_401k#:~:text=In%202020%2C%20there%20were%20about,of%20former%20employees%20and%20retirees.

must make sure they're putting money away for that day when they no longer work but still need income. To save for retirement, they may have to sacrifice their lifestyle during their work career, which isn't necessarily the case for those with employer-provided pensions.

Confidence can be another big differentiator. Retirees who receive pensions from companies that are solid and solvent can be relatively certain that their post-work checks will continue showing up month after month after month after month. . .forever until they pass away. Those who rely on 401(k)s and IRAs, on the other hand, may not be confident they saved enough through the years.

One of the most frequent questions we're asked is, "Do I have enough?" In other words, it isn't at all uncommon to see insecurity set in for those who have stopped receiving working wages and started taking money from finite pools of investments.

If there is anything to learn from this paradigm shift, it's that you must look out for yourself. Whether you have worked for a company for two years or twenty, you are still the one who has to look out for your own best interests. That holds doubly true when it comes to preparing for retirement. If you are one of the lucky ones who still has a pension, good for you. But for the rest of us, it is likely a 401(k)—or possibly one of its nonprofit- or government-sector counterparts, a 403(b) or 457 plan—is one of your biggest assets for retirement.

Some employers offer incentives to contribute to their company plans, like a company match. On that subject, I have one thing to say: *Do it!* Nothing in life is free, as they say, but a company match on your retirement funds is about as close to free money as it gets. If you can make the minimum to qualify for your company's match at all, go for it.

Now, it's likely, during our working years, we mostly "set and forget" our 401(k) funding. Because it is tax-advantaged, your employer is taking money from your paycheck—before taxes—and putting it into your plan for you. Maybe you got to pick a selection of investments, or maybe your company only offers one choice of investment in your 401(k). Either way, while you are gainfully employed, your most impactful decision may just be the decision to continue funding your plan in the first place. But, when you are ready to retire or move jobs, you have choices to make requiring a little more thought and care.

When you are ready to part ways with your job, you have a few options:

- Leave the money where it is
- Take the cash (and pay income taxes and perhaps a 10 percent additional federal tax if you are younger than age fifty-nine-and-one-half)
- Transfer the money to another employer plan (if the new plan allows)
- Roll the money over into a self-directed IRA

Now, these are just general options. You will have to decide, hopefully with the help of a retirement planner, what's right for you. For instance, 401(k)s are typically pretty closely tied to the companies offering them, so when changing jobs, it may not always be possible to transfer a 401(k) to another 401(k). Leaving the money where it is may also be out of the question—some companies have direct cash payout or rollover policies once someone is no longer employed.

Also, remember what we mentioned earlier about how we change jobs more often these days? That means you likely have a 401(k) with your current company, but you may also have a string of retirement accounts trailing you from other jobs.

Just last year, we saw an example of this when a client brought in a letter they had received from Social Security. The letter stated that the individual had a pension with a company where they'd worked more than fifteen years earlier. Before receiving the letter, the client had forgotten all about it. That's what tends to happen when life and new job opportunities and all sorts of other distractions get in our way. The truth is, we encounter scenarios like this a few times a year.

It's easy to understand why, too: Moving money from an employer plan can be both complicated and confusing. It also can be costly if you don't do it in a tax-efficient or proper manner.

What's more, once you move it out of an employer plan, you must decide where to put it and how to invest it. For many, it's just easier to leave the money behind and think about it another day.

When we help families with these concerns and consolidate money into one IRA—rather than leaving money floating in a variety of employer plans and accounts—they're relieved and appreciative. Those feelings only grow stronger as they age, when simplicity begins to look even more attractive.

When it comes to your retirement income, it's important to be able to pull together *all* your assets, so you can examine what you have and where, and then decide what you will do with it.

Tax-Qualified, Tax-Preferred, Tax-Deferred ... Still TAXED

Financial media often cite IRAs and 401(k)s for their tax benefits. After all, with traditional plans, you put your money in, pre-tax, and it hopefully grows for years, even decades, untaxed. That's why these accounts are called "tax-qualified" or "tax-deferred" assets. They aren't *tax-free!* Rarely does Uncle Sam allow business to continue without receiving his piece of the pie, and your retirement assets are no different. If you didn't pay taxes on the front end, you will pay taxes on the money you withdraw from these accounts in retirement. Don't get me wrong: This isn't an inherently good or bad thing; it's just the way it is. It's important to understand, though, for the sake of planning ahead.

In retirement, many people assume they will be in a lower tax bracket. Are you planning to pare down your lifestyle in retirement? Perhaps you are, and perhaps you will have substantially less income in retirement. But many of my clients tell me they want to live life more or less the same as they always have. The money they would previously have spent on business attire or gas for their commute they now want to spend on hobbies and grandchildren. That's all fine, and for many of them, it is doable, but does it put them in a lower tax bracket? Probably not.

Keep in mind, IRAs, 401(k)s, and their alternatives have a few limitations because of their special tax status. For one thing, the IRS sets limits on your contributions to these retirement accounts. If you are contributing to a 401(k) or an equivalent nonprofit or government plan, your annual contribution limit is $22,500 (as of 2023). If you are fifty or older, the IRS allows additional contributions, called "catch-up contributions," of up to $7,500 on top of the regular limit of $22,500. For an IRA, the limit is $6,500, with a catch-up limit of an additional $1,000.[41] Beginning in 2024, catch-up contributions for individuals with income exceeding $145,000 must transfer into a Roth IRA.[42]

Because their tax advantages come from their intended use as retirement income, withdrawing funds from these accounts before you turn fifty-nine-and-one-half can carry stiff penalties. In addition to fees your investment management company might charge, you will have to pay income tax *and* a 10 percent federal tax penalty, with few exceptions.

The fifty-nine-and-one-half rule for retirement accounts is incredibly important to remember, especially when you're young. Younger workers are often tempted to cash out an IRA from a previous employer and then are surprised to find their checks missing 20 percent of the account value to income taxes, penalty taxes, and account fees.

Many millennials I see in my practice say, while they may be socking money away in their workplace retirement plan, it is

---

[41] IRS.gov. December 8, 2022. "401(k) limit increases to $22,500 for 2023, IRA limit rises to $6,500" https://www.irs.gov/newsroom/401k-limit-increases-to-22500-for-2023-ira-limit-rises-to-6500
[42] Fidelity.com. 2023. "SECURE 2.0: Rethinking retirement savings" https://www.fidelity.com/learning-center/personal-finance/secure-act-2

often the *only* place they are saving. This could be problematic later because of the fifty-nine-and-one-half rule; what if you have an emergency? It is important to fund your retirement, but you need to have some liquid assets handy as emergency funds. This can help you avoid breaking into your retirement accounts and incurring taxes and penalties because of the fifty-nine-and-one-half rule.

RMDs

Remember how we talked about the 401(k) or IRA being a "tax wrapper" for your funds? Well, eventually, Uncle Sam will want a bite of that candy bar. So, when you turn seventy-three, the government requires you withdraw a portion of your account, which the IRS calculates based on the size of your account and your estimated lifespan. This required minimum distribution, or RMD, is the government's insurance it will collect some taxes, at some point, from your earnings. Because you didn't pay taxes on the front end, you will now pay income taxes on whatever you withdraw, including your RMDs.

Let me reiterate something I pointed out in the Longevity chapter. Beginning at age seventy-three, you are required to withdraw a certain minimum amount every year from your 401(k) or IRA, or else you will face a tax penalty on any RMD monies you should have withdrawn but didn't—and that's on top of income tax. The SECURE Act 2.0 reduced the penalty to 25 percent (from 50 percent). Timely corrections also can reduce the penalty to 10 percent.[43]

Even after you begin RMDs, you can still also continue contributing to your 401(k) or IRAs if you are still employed, which can affect the whole discussion on RMDs and possible tax considerations. The SECURE Act 2.0 raised the RMD age to seventy-three from seventy-two. In addition, the latest

---

[43] Jim Probasco. Investopedia.com. January 6, 2023. "SECURE 2.0 Act of 2022." https://www.investopedia.com/secure-2-0-definition-5225115

legislation stipulates the RMD age will increase to seventy-five for those turning seventy-four after December 31, 2032.[44]

If you don't need income from your retirement accounts, RMDs can seem like more of a tax burden than an income boon. While some people prefer to reinvest their RMDs, this comes with the possibility of additional taxation: You'll pay income taxes on your RMDs and then potential capital gains taxes on the growth of your investments. If you are legacy-minded, there are other ways to use RMDs, many of which have tax benefits.

SECURE 2.0 Act provisions

In addition to changes imposed for RMD ages, Secure Act 2.0 also expanded access to retirement savings using different methods. Provisions in the legislation go into effect at different times, ranging from 2023-25.

- Beginning January 2, 2024, plan participants can access up to $1,000 (once a year) from retirement savings for emergency personal or family expenses without paying a 10 percent early withdrawal penalty.
- Beginning January 2, 2024, employees can establish a Roth emergency savings account of up to $2,500 per participant.
- Beginning January 2, 2024, domestic abuse survivors can withdraw the lesser of $10,000 or 50 percent of their retirement account without penalty.
- Beginning January 1, 2023, victims of a qualified, federally declared disaster can withdraw up to $22,000 from their retirement account without penalty.[45]

Permanent Life Insurance

One way to turn those pesky RMDs into a legacy is through permanent life insurance. Assuming you need the death benefit coverage and can qualify for it medically, if properly structured,

---

[44] Ibid.
[45] Betterment.com. January 12, 2023. "SECURE Act 2.0: Signed into Law" https://www.betterment.com/work/resources/secure-act-2

these products can pass on a sizeable death benefit to your beneficiaries, tax-free, as part of your general legacy plan.

ILIT

Another way to use RMDs toward your legacy is to work with an estate planning attorney to create an irrevocable life insurance trust (ILIT). This is basically a permanent life insurance policy placed within a trust. Because the trust is irrevocable, you would relinquish control of it, but, unlike with just a permanent life insurance policy, your death benefit won't count toward your taxable estate.

Annuities

Because annuities can be tax-deferred, using all or a portion of your RMDs to fund an annuity contract can be one way to further delay taxation while guaranteeing your income payments (either to you or your loved ones) later. Of course, this assumes you don't need the RMD income during your retirement.

Qualified Charitable Distributions

If you are charity-minded, you may use your RMDs toward a charitable organization instead of using them for income. You must do this directly from your retirement account (you can't take the RMD check and *then* pay the charity) for your withdrawals to be qualified charitable distributions (QCDs), but this is one way of realizing some of the benefits of a charitable legacy during your own lifetime. You will not need to pay taxes on your QCDs, and they won't count toward your annual charitable tax deduction limit, plus you'll be able to see how the organization you are supporting uses your donations. You should consult a retirement planner on how to correctly make a QCD.

Roth IRA

Since the Taxpayer Relief Act of 1997, there has been a different kind of retirement account, or "tax wrapper," available to the public: the Roth. Roth IRAs and Roth 401(k)s each differ from their traditional counterparts in one big way: You pay your taxes on the front end. This means, once your post-tax money is in the Roth account, as long as you follow the rules and limitations of that account, your distributions are truly tax-free. You won't pay income tax when you take withdrawals, so, in turn, you don't have to worry about RMDs. However, Roth accounts have similar limitations as traditional 401(k)s and IRAs when it comes to withdrawing earnings before age fifty-nine-and-one-half, with the added stipulation that the account must have been open for at least five years in order for the account holder to make withdrawals.

As previously mentioned, Roth conversions can be a big part of a tax plan. We build our clients' tax plans taking into consideration their entire projected retirement with special consideration for the current year and the following year, and we do this annually.

If a Roth conversion makes sense, we will recommend it. If it makes sense to withhold taxes from the conversion, we will recommend that, too.

Our clients don't have to worry about the mechanics of the conversions. They don't even have to worry about bringing it to us as a potential strategy. We bring it up proactively and evaluate the benefits of the conversion for them well in advance. Their written plan will show whether a conversion makes sense and, if so, how much should be converted.

Taking Charge

As mentioned earlier, the 401(k) and IRA have largely replaced pensions, but they aren't an equal trade.

Pensions are employer-funded; the money feeding into them is money that wouldn't ever show up on your pay stub. Because 401(k)s are self-funded, you must actively and consciously save. This distinction has made a difference when it comes to funding retirement. Fidelity Investments published a story detailing that the average 401(k) balance for a person age fifty-five to sixty-four is $189,800, but the median likely tells the full story. The median 401(k) balance for a person age fifty-five to sixty-four is $56,450. Those figures reflect Fidelity accounts from the third quarter of 2022.[46]

There can be many reasons why people underfund their retirement plans, like being overwhelmed by the investment choices or taking withdrawals from IRAs when they leave an employer. Still, the reason at the top of the list is this: People simply aren't participating to begin with.

So, whether you use a 401(k) with an employer or an IRA alternative with a private company, separate from your workplace, the most important retirement savings decision you can make is to sock away your money somewhere in the first place.

---

[46] Arielle O'Shea. Nerd Wallet. December 22, 2022. "The Average 401(k) Balance by Age" https://www.nerdwallet.com/article/investing/the-average-401k-balance-by-age

CHAPTER 7

Annuities

In my practice, I offer my clients a variety of products—from securities to insurance—all designed to help them reach their financial goals. You may be wondering: Why single out one product in this book?

Well, while most of my clients have a pretty good understanding of business and finance, I sometimes find those who have the impression there must be magic involved. Some people assume there is a magic finance wand we can wave to change years' worth of savings into a strategy for retirement income. But it's not as easy as a goose laying golden eggs or the Fairy Godmother turning a pumpkin into a coach!

Finances aren't magic; it takes lots of hard work and, typically, several financial products and strategies to pull together a complete retirement plan. Of all the financial products I work with, it seems people find none more mysterious than annuities. And, if I may say, even some of those who recognize the word "annuity" have a limited understanding of the product. So, in the interest of demystifying annuities, let me tell you a little about what an annuity is.

In general, insurance is a financial hedge against risk. Car owners buy auto insurance to protect their finances in case they injure someone or someone injures them. Homeowners have house insurance to protect their finances in case of a fire, flood, or another disaster. People have life insurance to protect their finances in case of untimely death. Almost juxtaposed to life insurance, people have annuities in case of a long life; annuities can give you financial protection by providing consistent and reliable income payments.

The basic premise of an annuity is you, the annuitant, pay an insurance company some amount in exchange for their contractual guarantee they will pay you income for a certain time period. How that company pays you, for how long, and how much they offer are all determined by the annuity contract you enter into with the insurance company.

How You Get Paid

There are two ways for an annuity contract to provide income: The first is through what is called annuitization, and the second is through the use of income riders. We'll get into income riders in a bit, but let's talk about annuitization. That nice, long word is, in my opinion, one reason annuities have a reputation for mystery and misinformation.

Annuitization

When someone "annuitizes" a contract, it is the point where he or she turns on the income stream. Once a contract has been annuitized, there is no going back. With annuities, if the policyholder lives longer than the insurance company planned, the insurance company is still obligated to pay him or her, even if the payments end up being way more than the contract's actual value. If, however, the policyholder dies an untimely death, depending on the contract type, the insurance company may keep anything left of the money that funded the annuity— nothing would be paid out to the contract holder's survivors. You see where that could make some people balk? Now, modern annuities rarely rely on annuitization for the income portion of the contract, and instead have so many bells and whistles that the old concept of annuitization seems outdated, but because this is still an option, it's important to at least understand the basic concept.

Riders

Speaking of bells and whistles, let's talk about riders. Modern annuities have a lot of different options these days, many in the form of riders you can add to your contract for a fee—usually about 1 percent of the contract value per year. Each rider has its particulars, and the types of riders available will vary by the type of annuity contract purchased, but I'll just briefly outline some of these little extras:

- Lifetime income rider: Contract guarantees you an enhanced or flexible income for life
- Death benefit rider: Contract pays an enhanced death benefit to your beneficiaries even if you have annuitized
- Return of premium rider: Guarantees you (or your beneficiaries) will at least receive back the premium value of the annuity
- Long-term care rider: Provides a certain amount, sometimes as much as twice the normal income benefit amount for a period of time to help pay for long-term care if the contract holder is moved to a nursing home or assisted living situation

This isn't an extensive look, and usually the riders have fancier names based on the issuing company, like "Lorem Ipsum Insurance Company Income Preferred Bonus Fixed Index Annuity rider," but I just wanted to show you what some of the general options are in layperson's terms.

Types of Annuities

Annuities break down into four basic types: immediate, variable, fixed, and fixed index.

Immediate

Immediate annuities primarily rely on annuitization to provide income—you give the insurance company a lump sum up front, and your payments begin immediately. Once you begin receiving income payments, the transaction is irreversible, and you no longer have access to your money in a lump sum. When you die, any remaining contract value is typically forfeited to the insurance company.

All other annuity contract types are "deferred" contracts, meaning you fund your policy as a lump sum or over a period of years and you give it the opportunity to grow over time— sometimes years, sometimes decades.

Variable

A variable annuity is an insurance contract as well as an investment. It's sold by insurance companies, but only through someone who is registered to sell investment products. With a variable annuity contract, the insurance company invests your premiums in subaccounts that are tied to the stock market. This makes it a bit different from the other annuity contract types because it is the only contract where your money is subject to losses because of market declines. Your contract value has a greater opportunity to grow, but it also stands to lose. Additionally, your contract's value will be subject to the underlying investment's fees and limitations—including capital gains taxes, management fees, etc. Once it is time for you to receive income from the contract, the insurance company will pay you a certain income, locked in at whatever your contract's value was.

Fixed

A traditional fixed annuity is pretty straightforward. You purchase a contract with a guaranteed interest rate and, when you are ready, the insurance company will make regular income payments to you at whatever payout rate your contract guarantees. Those payments will continue for the rest of your life and, if you choose, for the remainder of your spouse's life.

Fixed annuities don't typically offer significant upside potential, but many people like them for their guarantees (after all, if your Aunt May lives to be ninety-five, knowing she has a paycheck later in life can be her mental and financial safety net), as well as for their predictability. Unlike variable annuities, which are subject to market risk and might be up one year and down the next, you can easily calculate the value of your fixed annuity over your lifetime.

Fixed Index

To recap, variable annuities take on more risk to offer more possibilities to grow. Fixed annuities have less potential growth, but they protect your principal. In the last couple of decades, many insurance companies have retooled their product line to offer fixed index annuities, which are sort of midway between variable and fixed annuities on that risk/reward spectrum. Fixed index annuities offer greater growth potential than traditional fixed annuities but less than variable annuities. Like traditional fixed annuities, however, fixed index annuities are protected from downside market losses.

Fixed index annuities earn interest that is tied to an external market index, meaning that, instead of your contract value growing at a set interest rate like a traditional fixed annuity, it has the potential to grow within a range. Your contract's value is credited interest based on the performance of an external market index like the S&P 500 while never being invested in the market itself. You can't invest in the S&P 500 directly, but each year, your annuity has the potential to earn interest based on the chosen index's performance, subject to limits set by the company such as caps, spreads, and participation rates.

For instance, if your contract caps your interest at 5 percent, then in a year that the S&P 500 gains 3 percent, your annuity value increases 3 percent. If the S&P 500 gains 35 percent, your annuity value gets a 5 percent interest bump. But since your money isn't actually invested in the market with a fixed index annuity, if the market nosedives (such as happened during 2000, 2008, , and 2022, anyone?) you won't see any increase in your contract value. Conversely, there will also be no decrease in your contract value—no matter how badly the market performed, as long as you follow the terms of the contract, you won't lose any of the interest you were credited in previous years.

So, what if the S&P 500 shows a market loss of 30 percent? Your contract value isn't going anywhere (unless you purchased an optional rider—this charge will still come out of your annuity value each year). For those who are more interested in protection than growth potential, fixed index annuities can be an attractive option because, when the stock market has a long period of positive performance, a fixed index annuity can enjoy conservative growth. And, during stretches where the stock market is erratic and stock values across the board take significant losses? Fixed index annuities won't lose anything due to the stock market volatility.

Occasionally, people will tell us annuities are bad. When we ask why, we'll sometimes hear, "I don't know; I just heard you should never buy an annuity."

The simple truth is, as with most things in life, there is a time and a place for everything. We use FIAs in our practice, but like any product we use, an FIA isn't a one-size-fits-all solution. Not all annuities are good—and even good annuities aren't ideal for every circumstance or person. We find the right annuity and use it in the right situation for the right person.

This approach really is no different than stocks. Not all stocks are good—and even good stocks aren't right for everyone.

That's why the customization of a portfolio is so important. We build the retirement plan first to know how much income is needed, how much investment risk is needed to achieve certain goals, and how much investment risk can be tolerated by the client. Then, when all the planning work is done, we create the portfolio together with that client.

The reality is many of our clients like FIAs because they provide certainty and confidence. Some of the FIAs we use not only provide principal guarantees, but also offer guaranteed income that clients don't have to worry about outliving. Instead of having a pension provided to you by an employer, this is like a pension you provide for yourself through a contract with an insurance company.

Other FIAs we use provide principal guarantees with reasonable upside potential. With these FIAs, when the market takes a hit, we can take a portion out of the FIA, roll it into clients' at-risk accounts and buy the market at a discount. This strategy works well because money that was protected in the FIA can be used to help provide upside when the markets begin to rebound. We often refer to this as "Go Time" with our clients because it gives them a strategy where they can take action and take advantage, capitalizing on market dips instead of just hanging on and riding out the downturns.

Other Things to Know About Annuities

We just talked about the four kinds of annuity contracts available, but all of them have some commonalities as annuities.

For all annuities, the contractual guarantees are only as strong as the insurance company that sells the product, which makes it important to thoroughly check the credit ratings of any company whose products you are considering.

Annuities are tax-deferred, meaning you don't have to pay taxes on interest earnings each year as the contract value grows. Instead, you will pay ordinary income taxes on your withdrawals. These are meant to be long-term products, so, like other tax-deferred or tax-advantaged products, if you begin taking withdrawals from your contract before age fifty-nine-and-one-half, you may also have to pay a 10 percent federal tax penalty. Also, while annuities are generally considered illiquid, most contracts allow you to withdraw up to 10 percent of your contract value every year. Withdraw any more, however, and you could incur additional surrender penalties.

Keep in mind, your withdrawals will deplete the accumulated cash value, death benefit, and, possibly, the rider values of your contract.

Annuities might not be for everyone, but they do have a place for many investors and retirees. As I mentioned a moment ago, this can be especially true following prolonged market dives.

Consider the stock dips we saw during the first half of 2020 and throughout much of 2022. During each of those periods, we had numerous clients implement the "Go Time" strategy I noted previously.

In 2020, for instance, some of our clients gladly took advantage of the "buy-low" opportunity they saw when the S&P 500 dropped by 34 percent in twenty-two days. They capitalized by moving money that had been in their FIA to the at-risk side of their portfolio. When the market reversed course and started to climb again, they made a lot with money that never was affected by the market's drop in the first place.

Many of those clients and others employed that same "Go Time" strategy again in 2022 when the markets suffered.

The bottom line is it's important to understand annuities before saying "yea" or "nay" on whether they fit into your plan; otherwise, you're not operating with complete information, wouldn't you agree? Regardless, you should talk to a retirement planner who can help you understand annuities, help you dissect your particular financial needs, and help show you whether an annuity is appropriate for your retirement plan.

CHAPTER 8

Estate & Legacy

I n my practice, I devote a significant portion of my time to matters of estates. That doesn't mean drawing up wills or trusts or putting together powers of attorney or anything like that. After all, I'm not an estate planning attorney. But I am a retirement planner, and what part of the "estate" isn't affected by money matters?

I've included this chapter because I have seen many people do estate planning wrong. Clients, or clients' families, have come in after experiencing a death in the family and have found themselves in the middle of probate, high taxes, or a discovery of something unforeseen (often long-term care) draining the estate.

I have also seen people do estate planning right: clients or families who visit my office to talk about legacies and how to make them last and adult children who have room to grieve without an added burden of unintended costs, without stress from a family ruptured because of inadequate planning.

I'll share some of these stories here. However, I'm not going to give you specific advice, since everyone's situation is unique. I only want to give you some things to think about and to underscore the importance of planning ahead.

I also will tell you that our team here at Merkle Retirement Planning does have relationships with estate planning attorneys. We will also work with our clients' personal attorneys, as long as the attorney specializes in estate planning and does a good job.

If our clients don't have a relationship with an estate planning attorney, we'll introduce them to an attorney we trust, have used, and vetted.

You Can't Take It With You

When it comes to legacy and estate planning, the most important thing is to *do it*. I have heard people from clients to celebrities (rap artist Snoop Dogg comes to mind) say they aren't interested in what happens to their assets when they die because they'll be dead. That's certainly one way to look at it. But I think that's a very selfish way to go about things—we all have people and causes we care about, and those who care about us. Even if the people we love don't *need* what we leave behind, they can still be fined or legally tied up in the probate process or burial costs if we don't plan for those. And that's not even considering what happens if you become incapacitated at some point while you are still alive. Having a plan in place can greatly reduce the stress of those responsibilities on your loved ones; it's just a loving thing to do.

Documents

There are a few documents that lay the groundwork of legacy planning. You've probably heard of all or most of them, but I'd like to review what they are and how people commonly use them. These are all things you should talk about with an estate planning attorney to establish your legacy.

Powers of Attorney

A power of attorney, or POA, is a document giving someone the authority to act on your behalf and in your best interests. These come in handy in situations where you cannot be present (think a vacation where you get stuck in Canada) or, for durable powers of attorney, even when you are incapacitated (think in a coma or coping with dementia).

It is important to have powers of attorney in place and to appoint someone you trust to act on your behalf in these matters. Have you ever heard of someone who was incapacitated after a car accident, whether from head trauma or being in a coma for weeks—sometimes months? Do you think their bills stopped coming due during that time? I like my phone company and my bank, but neither one is about to put a moratorium on sending me bills, particularly not for an extended or interminable period. A power of attorney would have the authority to pay your mortgage or cancel your cable while you are unable.

You can have multiple POAs and require them to act jointly.

What this looks like: Do you think two heads are better than one? One man, Chris, significantly relied on his two sons' opinions for both his business and personal matters. He appointed both sons as joint POA, requiring both their signoffs for his medical and financial matters. This can work well for some people, but many estate planning attorneys will caution you against this option. In this example, if Chris' two sons don't get along or can't come to an agreement on certain decisions, then making any decisions can become problematic.

You can have multiple POAs who can act independently.

What this looks like: Irene had three children with whom she routinely stayed. They lived in different areas of the country, which she thought was an advantage; one month she might be hiking out West, the next she could enjoy the newest off-Broadway production, and the next she could soak up some Southern sun. She named her three children as independently authorized POAs, so, if something happened, no matter where she was, the child closest could step in to act on her behalf.

You can have POAs who have different responsibilities.

What this looks like: Although Luke's friend Claire, a nurse, was his go-to and POA for health-related issues, financial matters usually made her nervous, so he appointed his good neighbor, Matt, as his POA in all of his financial and legal matters.

In addition to POAs, it may be helpful to have an advanced medical directive. This is a document where you have pre-decided what choices you would make about different health scenarios. An advanced medical directive can help ease the burden for your medical POA and loved ones, particularly when it comes to end-of-life care.

Wills

Perhaps the most basic document of legacy planning, a will is a legal document wherein you outline your wishes for your estate. When it comes to your estate after your death, having a will is the foundation of your legacy. Without one, your loved ones are left behind, guessing what you would have wanted, and the court will likely split your assets according to the state's defaults. Maybe that's exactly what you wanted, as far as anyone knows, right? Because even if you told your nephew he could have your car he's been driving, if it's not in writing, it still might go to the brother, sister, son, or daughter to whom you aren't speaking.

However, it may not be enough just to have a will. Even with a will, your assets will be subject to probate. Probate is what we call the state's process for determining a will's validity. A judge will go through your will to question if it conflicts with state law, if it is the most up-to-date document, if you were mentally competent at the time it was in order, etc. For some, this is a quick, easily-resolved process. For others, particularly if someone steps forward to contest the will, it may take years to settle, all the while subjecting the assets to court costs and attorney's fees.

One other undesirable piece of the probate process is that it is a public process. That means anyone can go to the courthouse, ask for copies of the case, and discover your assets. They can also see who is slated to receive what and who is disputing.

Look, the last thing any of us want to do is be a burden to our loved ones after we die. Unfortunately, that happens all too often.

A few years ago, I met a gentleman who spent months trying to navigate the legal maze of the probate process after his wife had passed away. She'd had two separate 401(k) plans, each worth about $500,000, but neither plan named a beneficiary.

For three months, this man had been trying to find his way through the legal probate protocol for taking ownership of both plans. Up to that point, he had been unsuccessful. As one would expect, he grew increasingly frustrated by the amount of time, thought, and energy his efforts consumed.

And let's not forget, he had just lost his best friend and was still working through all the emotional anguish associated with that painful event.

If only his wife had listed him as a beneficiary, the accounts would have transferred to him seamlessly outside of probate, causing him much less stress and strain.

That's why it's so important to remember that beneficiary lines trump wills. So, that large life insurance policy? What if, when you bought it fifteen years ago, you wrote your ex-husband's name on the beneficiary line? Even if you stipulate otherwise in your will, the company that holds your policy will pay out to your ex-spouse. Or, how about the thousands of dollars in your IRA you dedicated to the children thirty years ago, but one of your children was killed in a car accident, leaving his wife and two toddlers behind? That IRA could transfer to your remaining children, with nothing for your daughter-in-law and grandchildren.

That may paint a grim portrait, but I can't underscore enough the importance of working with a skilled estate planning attorney to keep your will and beneficiary lines up to date as your life changes.

Trusts

Another piece of legacy planning to consider is the trust.

A trust is set up through an attorney and allows a third party, or trustee, to hold your assets and determine how they will pass to your beneficiaries. Many people are skeptical of trusts because they assume trusts are only appropriate for the fabulously wealthy.

However, a simple trust will likely cost a little more than $1,000 if prepared by an attorney, and fees can be higher for couples.[47] But a trust can help you avoid both the expense and publicity of probate, provide a more immediate transfer of wealth, avoid some taxes, and provide you greater control over your legacy.

For instance, if you want to set aside some funds for a grandchild's college education, you can make it a requirement he or she enrolls in classes before your trust will dispense any funds. Like a will, beneficiary lines will override your trust conditions, so you must still keep insurance policies and other assets up to date.

Like any financial or legal consideration, there are many options these days beyond the simple "yes or no" question of whether to have a trust. For one thing, you will need to consider if you want your trust to be revocable (you can change the terms while you are alive) or irrevocable (can't be changed; you are no longer the "owner" of the contents). A brief note here about

---

[47] Rickie Houston. smartasset.com. August 31, 2022. "How Much Does It Cost to Set Up a Trust? https://smartasset.com/estate-planning/how-much-does-it-cost-to-set-up-a-trust

irrevocable trusts: Although they have significant and greater tax benefits, they are still subject to a Medicaid look-back period. This means, if you transfer your assets into an irrevocable trust in an attempt to shelter them from a Medicaid spend-down, you will be ineligible for Medicaid coverage of long-term care for five years. Yet, an irrevocable trust can avoid both probate and estate taxes, and it can even protect assets from legal judgments against you.

Another thing to remember when it comes to trusts, in general, is, even if you have set up a trust, you must remember to fund it. In my twenty-four years' work, I've had numerous clients come to me, assuming they have protected their assets with a trust. When we talk about taxes and other pieces of their legacy, it turns out they never retitled any assets or changed any paperwork on the assets they wanted in the trust. So, please remember, a trust is just a bunch of fancy legal papers if you haven't followed through on retitling your assets.

Taxes

Although charitable contributions, trusts, and other tax-efficient strategies can reduce your tax bill, it's unlikely your estate will be passed on entirely tax-free. Yet, when it comes to building a legacy that can last for generations, taxes can be one of the heaviest drains on the impact of your hard work.

For 2023, the federal estate exemption was $12.92 million per individual and $25.84 million for a married couple, with estates facing up to a 40 percent tax rate after that. Currently, the new estate limits are set to increase with inflation until January 1, 2026, when they will "sunset" back to the inflation-adjusted 2017 limits.[48] And that's not taking into account the various state regulations and taxes regarding estate and inheritance transfers.

---

[48] IRS.gov. December 20, 2022. "What's New — Estate and Gift Tax" https://www.irs.gov/businesses/small-businesses-self-employed/whats-new-estate-and-gift-tax

Another tax concern "frequent flyer": retirement accounts.

Your IRA or 401(k) can be a source of tax issues when you pass away. For one thing, taking funds from a sizeable account can trigger a large tax bill. However, if you leave the assets in the account, minimum distributions (RMDs) are still required, which will take effect even after you die. If you pass the account to your spouse, he or she can keep taking your RMDs as is, or they can retitle the account in their name and receive RMDs based on their life expectancy. Remember, if you don't take your RMDs, the IRS will take up to 25 percent of your required distribution (10 percent if corrections are made in a timely fashion), and you will still have to pay income taxes whenever you withdraw that money.

Provisions in the original SECURE Act deem that anyone who inherits your IRA, with few exceptions (your spouse, a beneficiary less than ten years younger, or a disabled adult child, to name a few), will need to empty the account within ten years of your death.

Also—and this is a pretty big also—check with an attorney if you are considering making your trust the beneficiary of your IRA or 401(k) plan. An improperly titled beneficiary form for the IRA or poorly constructed trust could mean a difference of thousands of dollars in taxes. This is just one more reason to work with a retirement planner who can strategically partner with an estate planning attorney to diligently work through your options.

CHAPTER 9

Women Retire Too

I help men, women, and families from all walks of life on their journey to and through retirement. Yet, we want to address the female demographic specifically. Why? To be perfectly blunt, women are more likely to deal with poverty than men when they reach retirement.

In 2021, the overall poverty rate for women slightly exceeded the rate for men, but among those seventy-five years and older, 13.51 percent of women lived at the poverty rate compared to 8.82 percent of men.[49]

The topics, products, and strategies I cover elsewhere in this book are meant to help address retirement concerns for men *and* women, but the dire statistic above is a reminder that much of traditional planning is geared toward men. Male careers, male lifespans, male health care. The bottom line is women's career paths often look much different than men's, so why would their retirement planning look the same?

Women often embrace different roles and values than men as workers, wives, mothers, and daughters. They are more apt to take on roles as caretakers. They often plan for events, worry about loved ones, tend to details, and think about the future. Also, they often want everything to be just right, and they want

---

49 statistica.com. 2023. "Poverty rate in the United States in 2021, by age and gender" https://www.statista.com/statistics/233154/us-poverty-rate-by-gender/

to be right themselves. It could be you've seen the following affixed to a decorative sign, refrigerator magnet, or T-shirt: "If I agreed with you, we'd both be wrong." The barb features a picture of a woman speaking to a man.

If these characteristics I listed about women are accurate, shouldn't they deserve special considerations from financial professionals? The case can be made, particularly since 69 percent of men in the U.S. age 65 and older happen to be married, compared to 47 percent of women in that age classification.[50] Single women cannot capitalize on the resource pooling and potential economies of scale accompanying a marriage or partnership.

Women, on average, also tend to live longer than men, something I'll address in greater detail in a moment. That means women not only often become caregivers for their spouses but also frequently need to care for themselves—or at least make provisions for future individual care needs.

Because women generally live longer, they often need more long-term care and need it for longer periods. You see the challenge here, right?

Add the fact that women, on average, make less than men over the course of their careers, and it's easy to see why planning for them can be more nuanced and more necessary.

Be Informed

It's a familiar scene in many financial offices across the country: A woman comes into an appointment carrying a sack full of unopened envelopes. Often through tears, she sits across the desk from a financial professional and apologizes her way through a conversation about what financial products she owns and where her income is coming from. She is recently widowed and was sure her spouse was taking care of the finances, but

---

[50] Administration for Community Living. November 30, 2022. "Profile of Older Americans." https://acl.gov/aging-and-disability-in-america/data-and-research/profile-older-americans

now she doesn't know where all their assets are kept, and her confidence in her financial outlook has wavered after walking through funeral expenses and realizing she's down to one income.

Often, she may be financially "okay." Yet, the uncertainty can be wearying, particularly when the family is already reeling from a loss. While this scenario sometimes plays out with men, in my experience, it's more likely to be a woman in that chair across from my desk, probably, in part, because of Western traditions about money management being "a guy thing." But it doesn't have to be this way. This all-too-common scenario can be wiped away with just a little preparation.

Talk to Your Spouse/ Work with a Retirement Planner

While there are many factors affecting women's financial preparation for and situation in retirement, I cannot emphasize enough that the decision to be informed, to be a part of the conversation, and to be aware of what is going on with your finances is absolutely paramount to a confident retirement.

With most of the couples I've seen, there is usually an "alpha" when it comes to finances. It isn't always men—for many of my coupled clients, the wife is the alpha who keeps the books and budgets and knows where all of the family's assets are, down to the penny—yet, statistically, among baby boomers it is usually a man who runs the books. But, as time goes on, it looks like the ratio of male to female financial alphas is evening out based on my experience working with couples.

The breakdown happens when there is a lack of communication, when no one other than the financial alpha knows how much the family has and where. In the end, it doesn't matter who handles the money; it's about all parties being informed of what's going on financially.

There are a lot of ways to open the conversation about money. One woman started a conversation with her husband, the financial alpha, by sitting down and saying, "Teach me how to be a widow." Perhaps that sounds grim, but it was to the point, and it spurred what she said was a very fruitful conversation. Couples sometimes have their first real conversation about money, assets, and their retirement income approach, in our office. The important thing about having these conversations isn't where, it's when . . . and the best "when" is as soon as possible.

She said the fruit of the weekend exercise they engaged in some twenty years earlier couldn't have been more apparent than when she ultimately accompanied a recently widowed friend of hers to a financial appointment. Her friend was emotional the whole time, afraid she would run out of money any day. The financial professional ultimately showed the friend that she was financially in good shape, but not before the friend had already spent months worried that each check would exhaust her bank account. That's no way to live after losing a loved one. It was preventable had her deceased spouse and financial professional included her in a conversation about "widowhood."

Spouse-Specific Options

One area where it might be especially important to be on the same page between spouses is when it comes to financial products or services that have spousal options. A few that come to mind are pensions and Social Security, although life insurance and annuity policies also have the potential to affect both spouses.

With pensions, taking the worker's life-only option is somewhat attractive—after all, the monthly payment is bigger. However, you and your spouse should discuss your options. When we're talking about both of you, as opposed to just one lifespan, there is an increased likelihood at least one of you will live a long, long time. This means the monthly payout will be less, but it also ensures that, no matter which spouse outlives the other, no one will have to suffer the loss of a needed pension paycheck in his or her later retirement years.

While we covered Social Security options in a different chapter, I think some of the spousal information bears repeating. Particularly, if you worked exclusively inside the home for a significant number of years, you may want to talk about taking your Social Security benefits based on your spouse's work history. After all, Social Security is based on your thirty-five highest-earning years.

Things to remember about the spousal benefits:[51]

- Your benefit will be calculated as a percentage (up to 50 percent) of your spouse's earned monthly benefit at his or her full retirement age, or FRA.
- For you to begin receiving a spousal benefit, your spouse must have already filed for his or her own benefits and you must be at least sixty-two.
- You can qualify for a full half of your spouse's benefits if you wait until you reach FRA to file.
- Beginning your benefits earlier than your FRA will reduce your monthly check but waiting to file until after FRA will not increase your benefits.

For divorcees:[52]

- You may qualify for an ex-spousal benefit if . . .
    a. You were married for a decade or more
    b. *and* you are at least sixty-two
    c. *and* you have been divorced for at least two years
    d. *and* you are currently unmarried
    e. *and* your ex-spouse is at least sixty-two (qualifies to begin taking Social Security)
- Your ex-spouse does not need to have filed for you to file on his or her benefit.

---

[51] Social Security Administration. "Retirement Planner: Benefits For You As A Spouse." https://www.ssa.gov/planners/retire/applying6.html
[52] Social Security Administration. "Retirement Planner: If You Are Divorced." https://www.ssa.gov/planners/retire/divspouse.html

- Similar to spousal benefits, you can qualify for up to half of your ex-spouse's benefits if you wait to file until your FRA.
- If your ex-spouse dies, you may file to receive a widow/widower benefit on his or her Social Security record as long as you are at least age sixty and fulfill all the other requirements on the preceding alphabetized list.
  a. This will not affect the benefits of your ex-spouse's current spouse

For widow's (or widower's, for that matter) benefits:[53]
- You may qualify to receive as much as your deceased spouse would have received if . . .
  a. You were married for at least nine months before his or her death
  b. *or* you would qualify for a divorced spousal benefit
  c. *and* you are at least sixty
  d. *and* you did not/have not remarried before age sixty
- You may earn delayed credits on your spouse's benefit *if* your spouse hadn't already filed for benefits when he or she died.
- Other rules may apply to you if you are disabled or are caring for a deceased spouse's dependent or disabled child.

Longevity

On average, women live longer than men. Most stats put average female longevity at about two years more than men. But averages are tricky things. An April 2022 report by the

---

[53] Social Security Administration. "Survivors Planner: If You Are The Worker's Widow Or Widower." https://www.ssa.gov/planners/survivors/ifyou.html#h2

World Economic Forum listed the eight oldest people in the world to all be women. They ranged in age from 118 years old to 114 and included two Americans.[54]

On one hand, this is a Brandi Chastain moment. You know, when the American soccer icon shed her jersey to celebrate a game-winning penalty kick to win the World Cup. Seriously, how fabulous are women? They tend to be meticulous, resolute, and perseverant. On the other hand, the trend for women to live longer presents longstanding financial ramifications.

Simply Needing More Money in Retirement

Living longer in retirement means needing more money, period. Barring a huge lottery win or some crazy stock market action, the date you retire is likely the point at which you have the most money you will ever have. Not to put too grim a spin on it, but the problem with longevity is, the further you get away from that date, the further your dollars have to stretch. If you planned to live to a nice eighty-something but live to a nice one-hundred-something, that is *two decades* you will need to account for, monetarily.

To put this in perspective, let's say you like to drink coffee as an everyday splurge. Not accounting for inflation or leap years, a $2.50 cup-a-day habit is $18,250 over a two-decade span. Now, think of all the things you like to do that cost money. Add those up for twenty years of unanticipated costs. I think you'll see what I mean.

During the 2020 onset of the coronavirus pandemic, many learned to cut costs. For some, that amounted to skipping their decadent latte. For others, however, cutbacks became acute. According to data compiled by Age Wave and Edward Jones, 32 percent of Americans plan to retire later than planned because of the pandemic. Women felt a more adverse effect. The report

---

54 Martin Armstrong. World Economic Forum. April 29, 2022. "How old are the world's oldest people?" https://www.weforum.org/agenda/2022/04/the-oldest-people-in-the-world/

stipulated that 41 percent of women continued to save for retirement, compared to 58 percent of men.[55]

More Health Care Needs

In addition to the cost of living for a longer lifespan is the fact aging, plain and simple, means more health care, and more health care means more money. Women are survivors. They suffer from the morbidity-mortality paradox, which states women suffer more non-fatal illnesses throughout their lifetime than men, who experience fewer illnesses but higher mortality.

Women have been found to seek treatment more often when not feeling well and emphasize staying healthy when older, according to studies. Survival, I believe, is on the side of the woman. However, surviving things, like cancer, also means more checkups later in life.

A statistical concern for women involves the prospect of long-term care. Long-term care for women lasts 3.7 years on average compared to 2.2 years for men.[56]

Widowhood

Not only do women typically live longer than their same-age male counterparts, they also stand a greater chance of living alone as they age. Some divorce, separate or never marry. Among those aged sixty-five and over, 33 percent of women live alone compared to 20 percent of men.[57]

---

[55] Megan Leonhardt. cnbc.com. June 16, 2021. "58% of men were able to continue saving for retirement during the pandemic—but only 41% of women were." https://www.cnbc.com/2021/06/16/why-pandemic-hit-womens-retirement-savings-more-than-mens.html

[56] Lindsay Modglin. singlecare.com. February 15, 2022. "Long-term care statistics 2022" https://www.singlecare.com/blog/news/long-term-care-statistics/

[57] statistica.com. November 23, 2022. "Share of senior households living alone in the United States 2020, by gender"

I don't write this to scare people; rather, I think it's fundamentally important to prepare my female clients for something that may be a startling, *but very likely,* scenario. At some point, most women will have to handle their financial situations on their own. A little preparation can go a long way, and having a basic understanding of your household finances and the "who, what, where, and how much" of your family's assets is incredibly useful—it can prevent a tragic situation from being more traumatic.

In my opinion, the financial services industry sometimes underserves women in these situations. Some financial professionals tend to alienate women, even when their spouses are alive. I've heard several stories of women who sat through meeting after meeting without their financial professional ever addressing a single question to them.

In our firm, when we work with couples, we work hard to make sure our retirement income strategies work for *both* people. No matter who the financial alpha is, it's important for everyone affected by a retirement strategy to understand it.

That's why we created a succession checklist. It's a pretty straightforward list of financial things that a widow (or widower) needs to do after a spouse passes away. It includes to-do items like canceling credit cards, removing the spouse's name from bank accounts, switching to the Social Security survivorship benefit, taking the spouse's name off the house, and much, much more.

We also created a grief group that is held once a month at our office. While both men and women can attend, more women take advantage of this support opportunity. The group is led by a certified grief counselor, giving those who are grieving the loss of a loved one access to an expert.

It also gives them a chance to become part of a small community of people who are experiencing similar emotions and dealing with similar challenges. As people age, their social

https://www.statista.com/statistics/912400/senior-households-living-alone-usa/

circles shrink, but we've seen plenty of new friendships grow from our grief group—and we're proud of that. You see, we want to take care of our clients financially *and* personally.

As part of that mission, we also established our Caregiving Circle. When someone is tasked with providing care for a spouse or loved one, they also experience a flood of emotions, some confusing and hard to process. Much like our grief group, the Caregiving Circle provides people with professional counseling as well as an empathetic team of supporters who can relate to their struggles, circumstances, and feelings.

Taxes

One of the often-unexpected aspects of widowhood is the tax bill. Many women continue similar lifestyles to the ones they shared with their spouses. This, in turn, means continuing to have a similar need for income. However, after the death of a spouse, their taxes will be calculated based on a single filer's income table, which is much less forgiving than the couple's tax rates. With proper planning, your retirement planner and tax advisor may be able to help you take the sting out of your new tax status.

Caregiving

Caregiving.org updates its national report about every five years. According to its findings released in 2020, of the 53 million caregivers providing unpaid, informal care for older adults, 61 percent are women. Among today's family caregivers, 61 percent work and 45 percent report some kind of financial impact from providing a loved one care and support.[58]

In addition to the financial burden created by caregiving responsibilities, women often devote many hours each day to duties such as housekeeping and looking after loved ones. So

---

[58] caregiving.org. 2020 Report. "Caregiving in the U.S. 2020." https://www.caregiving.org/caregiving-in-the-us-2020/

then, when can women find the time to focus long and hard on financial matters?

Unfortunately, the impact and hardships created by traditional roles for women typically do not account for Social Security benefit losses or the losses of health care benefits and retirement savings. This also doesn't account for maternity care, mothers who homeschool, or women who leave the workforce to care for their children in any way.

I don't repeat these statistics to scare you. Not only are unpaid family caregivers spending their time and energy taking care of others, but they're also putting their own money towards the cause. An AARP study found that three-quarters of family caregivers surveyed were spending an average of $7,242 a year on out-of-pocket caregiving costs.[59] Yet, I think the emotional value of the care many women provide their elderly relatives or neighbors cannot be quantified. So, to be clear, this shouldn't be taken as a "why not to provide caregiving" spiel. Instead, it should be seen as a call for "why to *prepare* for caregiving" or "how to lessen the financial and emotional burden of caregiving."

Funding Your Own Retirement

For these reasons, women need to be prepared to fund more of their own retirements. There are several savings options and products, including the spousal IRA. A spousal IRA is an IRA that a non-earning spouse can contribute to. This allows a non-earning spouse to still contribute to a retirement plan. This is something to consider, particularly for families where one spouse has dropped out of the workforce to care for a relative.

Also, if you find yourself in a caregiving role, talk to your employer's human resources department. Some companies have paid leave, special circumstances, or sick leave options you

---

[59] Nancy Kerr. AARP. June 29, 2021. " Family Caregivers Spend More Than $7,200 a Year on Out-of-Pocket Costs."
https://www.aarp.org/caregiving/financial-legal/info-2021/high-out-of-pocket-costs.html

could qualify for, making it easier to cope and helping you stay in the workforce longer.

Saving Money

Women need more money to fund their retirements, period. But this doesn't have to be a significant burden—often, women are better at saving, while usually taking less risk in their portfolios.[60] This gives me reason to believe, as women get more involved in their finances, families will continue to be better-prepared for retirement, both *his* and *hers*.

---

[60] Maurie Backman. The Motley Fool. March 4, 2021. "A Summary of 20 Years of Research and Statistics on Women in Investing." https://www.fool.com/research/women-in-investing-research/

CHAPTER 10

Finding a Financial
Professional

L eave it to a lawyer to cut straight to the chase. A little over
a year ago, my team and I were discussing our process,
which we outlined in the Preface, with an attorney during
a Connection Visit. Before we could finish, the gentleman
interjected.

"You know," he said matter-of-factly, "it seems to me like
once we get this retirement plan set up, I really won't need you
guys anymore."

Believe it or not, I loved the candor. After all, it's rare to see
someone level with you to that degree. Furthermore, I can
completely understand why he—or anyone, for that matter—
would be tempted to think that way.

But here's the thing: Lives change. Times change. Inflation
and economies and markets and policymakers and regulations
change. That means plans are consistently changing too. In
much the same way that you should consult a doctor if you
experience a serious health issue, you also need to have a
seasoned retirement planner on your side when you encounter
an unexpected financial change or life crisis.

We told him that, of course, explaining how we likely would
need to make many adjustments and perform regular reviews
to protect him throughout his retirement journey. We told him

that our job was to help safeguard his finances, his family, and his future.

We also shared one of the most valuable lessons I learned in college—that you don't know what you don't know. When I attended Central College to study business management and marketing, I soon realized there was a whole world out there that I hadn't been exposed to while growing up more than two hours away in the tiny town of Central City. If I was going to excel, in academics or athletics, it quickly became apparent that I had a bunch of lessons to learn while sharpening my skills.

I think about that often when visiting with pre-retirees. Why? Because you only want to retire once. You have but one chance to get it right and retire your way.

At Merkle Retirement Planning, we serve a host of brilliant, accomplished individuals—people very much like the attorney; people who are dedicated, decorated, and discerning but simply haven't had to tackle the issues we've discussed in this book. They've never had to sort through the Social Security maze. Never had to figure out how to live on a portfolio when the markets are imploding. Never had to deal with Medicare, long-term care, wills, or trusts. They're great at what they do; they just don't know what they don't know, and we hear them admit as much quite often.

That, in a nutshell, is the value of working with a qualified retirement planner. It's why that attorney—the same gentleman who at first was unsure and uneasy about partnering with us—remains a client today. He now very much understands that there is significant value in the knowledge and experience we possess and in having a personal relationship with our team, which has your back and proactively works on your behalf because we genuinely care.

****

Don't underestimate that last sentence when you're looking for a retirement planner—and perhaps any professional. Always find someone who cares; someone who is both educated *and* empathetic. I simply can't stress that enough.

As I noted in the opening chapter, we're interested in communities, not customers, here at Merkle Retirement Planning. We believe business will take care of itself if we first develop real relationships and support our clients with far more than financial matters. We want to establish ties and earn trust, not just execute transactions.

I firmly believe that relationships can only grow so much within the walls of an office, so we continually seek ways to better connect with those we serve. We've done that from the moment Merkle Retirement Planning was founded in 2011. To truly get to know our clients and their goals, dreams, needs, concerns, and preferences, our team engages with them regularly outside our walls.

From hosting fun monthly appreciation events through a unique initiative called our Elevated Living Series to creating support groups for caregivers and those who recently experienced a loss, we do life with our clients as much as we do business with them. We take them and their friends or family ballroom dancing and to yoga and crafting classes. We invite them on nature walks and tours of breweries, museums, and the state Capitol. We go to ballgames and tailgating parties together. We do all that and more.

We also open the doors of our state-of-the-art office to friends and our Des Moines-area community. Clients use our office for club meetings; community leaders use it for chamber gatherings and celebrations. We offer regular Lunch and Learns to inform clients and others about relevant financial topics and current events that could impact their retirement. We believe all of that is essential to being a good community partner, and that's important to us.

It's important to our clients, too, because it expands their social network and opportunities—and because it is another way of showing that we truly do care.

****

So, in addition to empathy, what should you look for in a financial professional? And better yet, how can you determine if someone really is the right fit for *you*?

This certainly won't be the most sophisticated or eloquent answer you'll ever hear or read, but my first piece of advice simply would be to go with your gut and determine whether you like the person. Believe it or not, the gut test is pretty darn reliable, especially for those of you who are nearing or already in retirement.

The fact is, if you're already retired or are considering retirement, you've been around a lot of people and benefited from a lot of experiences. Chances are you can spot the proverbial snake oil salesman in a matter of moments, if not seconds. You also probably can tell rather quickly if someone's values, lifestyle, and personality mesh with yours. That's every bit as important as their knowledge and experience because those traits affect your level of trust.

Beyond the gut, there are several key questions you should ask. For starters:

- If your portfolio includes investments, does the financial professional adhere to the fiduciary standard? In other words, will he or she always do what's in your very best interest and disclose any potential conflicts of interest?
- Does he or she offer comprehensive retirement planning that addresses lifestyle, income, investments, taxes, health care, and legacy strategies? Or, is he or she only concerned with investments and the markets?
- Do you have a clear understanding of how the professional is compensated and the fees you will pay?
- Does the advisor specialize in your current phase of life?

Most advisors concentrate solely on the accumulation phase. In other words, their lone focus is on long-term investments.

The problem with that is when you reach retirement, you enter the distribution phase. In this phase, you need an advisor who can help you identify reliable income streams, tax-efficient withdrawal strategies, legacy plans, and ways to protect yourself against potential threats such as prolonged market downturns and long-term health care issues. You also need someone who can help you optimize benefits such as Medicare and Social Security. This is why we call ourselves retirement planners, not financial advisors. When you approach retirement, you want to partner with someone who specializes in helping people transition from the working years to the retirement years and beyond. You want to work with a retirement planner.

For those of you who are within ten years of retiring, one of the easiest ways to determine whether you're working with a holistic retirement planner, and not simply an accumulation advisor, is to ask yourself if you have a written plan that details tax-planning and income-planning concepts. The bottom line is you shouldn't have to ask your advisor about those strategies; they should be brought to your attention proactively. If you must initiate a conversation about Social Security or tax optimization, chances are you're working with an accumulation advisor, not someone skilled in the nuances of retirement.

Your retirement planner should be equally open and assertive when discussing fees. Often, I'll meet people who have no idea what exactly they're paying their advisor. "You know, I asked my advisor how they are compensated, and he just kind of danced around it," I've heard them say.

At Merkle Retirement Planning, we talk about fees from the very first visit; prospective clients don't even have to ask about it. We not only explain our fee-based compensation structure, but we provide clients a document detailing what and how we get paid. We sign it, have clients sign it, and we can review it any time if they have questions.

We want to be completely transparent and honest in everything we do—including the issuance of fees—because trust always precedes transactions.

****

I started this chapter with a brief client story, and I'd like to end with one, too.

Two years ago, one of our longtime clients passed away far too early. He was only seventy-three, and his three daughters were his life. I know that because he spent virtually every review and interaction raving about his girls. He simply couldn't talk about them enough—about the times they shared, how much he cared, and how he wanted to make sure they'd be protected if something ever happened to him.

When that unfortunate, unexpected something did happen and his daughters came to see me, I shared many of the closed-door conversations I'd had with their dad—stories of his memories, deep devotion, and pride. It was an amazing, emotional experience for all of us. For me, it was a true pleasure to give them what their father always had wanted—financial security—but it was an even greater privilege to give them what they wanted—more of their dad's love and admiration for them.

So, if you want to know the secret to finding the right retirement planner, my answer is pretty straightforward: Just do what the father of those three wonderful women did:

- Find someone who makes you comfortable.
- Find someone you trust.
- Find someone who listens and doesn't forget.
- Find someone who shares your philosophies and values.
- Find someone who's qualified to help you pursue your dreams and goals.
- Find someone who follows through and is committed to *always* doing right by you.

In short, find someone who cares. . .about you, your family, and your future so you can **Retire Your Way.**

Acknowledgments

I would like to express my deepest gratitude to everyone on the Merkle Retirement Planning team. Your tireless commitment to excellence and unwavering dedication, talent, and passion are the driving force behind us being able to help so many families retire their way!

I would also like to thank the individuals and families that we serve for allowing us the opportunity to do what we love to do every single day.

About the Author

LOREN MERKLE
MERKLE RETIREMENT PLANNING

While Loren loves talking about stock market trends, diving deep into a tax strategy, or discussing how to build a recession-resistant retirement plan, his favorite moments have nothing to do with investments or numbers. The real joy comes when people want to talk about taking their kids to Disney World, their latest adventure in the RV, or a new hobby they've picked up in retirement. That's when he knows their retirement plan is working, because no matter what is happening with the stock markets or the economy, they are still living out their retirement vision.

How can they be so calm despite the always looming storms? Education. Loren's passion is providing tools and resources that educate pre-retirees and retirees on the decisions that go into retirement. Once they understand their options, they are on their way to building a retirement plan that will allow them to focus less on the stock market and more on having fun in retirement. It's why he wrote this book, has a TV show called *Retiring Today*, and a podcast of the same name. These are great resources for pre-retirees and retirees who want to get it right.

Loren was born in Michigan and grew up in eastern Iowa. He grew up loving team sports like baseball, football, and basketball. He excelled in athletics and went on to play football and study business at Central College in Pella, Iowa.

He still embraces the team mantra, taking a team approach to help people retire. When a comprehensive retirement plan, called Your Merkle Plan, is delivered to a family or an individual, several team members are a part of the process. From the first contact with the Client Experience team, to the paperwork and transfers with Client Servicing team, to strategy with the Retirement Planners, Loren takes a team approach with the goals of delivering the best experience possible for each pre-retiree or retiree.

Loren's passions outside of retirement center around his family. Camping is one of his favorite activities. Almost every year, he loads up the SUV for a long stay on Lake Michigan with his Mom, Dad, siblings, and all the kids. His daughter Jayce loves playing on the beach and running through the campgrounds each summer with her cousins. As happens with parents, his daughter's passion has become one of Loren's favorite activities. On weekends when he's not camping, you can often find him watching (and cheering) as his daughter competes in gymnastics.

Merkle
RETIREMENT PLANNING

Grimes
1860 SE Princeton Dr.
Grimes, Iowa 50111

Phone: 515.278.1006
Email: info@MerklePlan.com
Web: merkleretirementplanning.com

www.ingramcontent.com/pod-product-compliance
Lightning Source LLC
Chambersburg PA
CBHW060845220526
45466CB00003B/1252